Horney Bartender

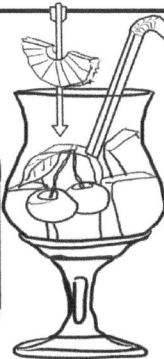

Cocktail Time
Cheers

Tequila

Southern Comfort

Rum

Spiced Rum

Old English Distillery
Sloe Gin

23% ALC/vol

Jack Daniel's
Tennessee
sour mash
Whiskey

Cranberry Juice

Rum

Spiced Rum

Old English Distillery
Sloe Gin

23% ALC/vol

1

by Really Thirsty

Lime Sour Bar Mix Recipe

- 1 Cup of Sugar
- 1 Cup of Water
- 1 Cup of freshly squeezed Lemon Juice
- 1/2 Cup of freshly squeezed Lime Juice
- Heat liquids on stove to dissolve sugar
- Let cool

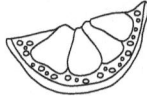

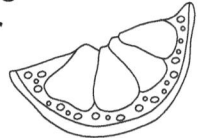

*Optional; add 2 egg whites... **Whipped** into your Sour Mix... to make Cocktail slightly foamy*

Simple Syrup Recipe

- *Add equal parts of Sugar and Water to a sauce pan and heat over Medium Heat*
- 1/2 Cup Sugar and 1/2 Cup Water
- Stir until Sugar is dissolved... about 1-2 minutes... Remove from heat when sugar is dissolved...
- Cool to room temperature...
- Store in the refrigerator.

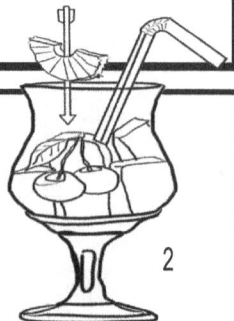

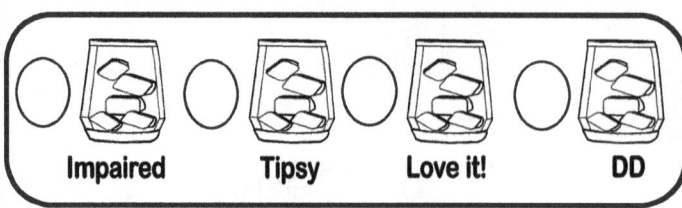

| Impaired | Tipsy | Love it! | DD |

Margarita Salty Rim Recipe

- Zest of 1 Lemon (*Optional*)
- Zest of 1 Lime
- 2 Tbs Salt (Pink Himalayan)
- Sprinkle Salt wide on a plate with an even layer... Sprinkle in your Lemon Zest and Lime Zest...
- Slowly with your fingers take the Lime Wedge ... gently go around the Margarita rim until perfectly moisten...
- Gently grab the rim of the Margarita Glass and tilt into salty Margarita Salty mixture

Impaired   Tipsy   Love it!   DD

Don't
Drink and Drive
Stop

3

Easy to Find Items

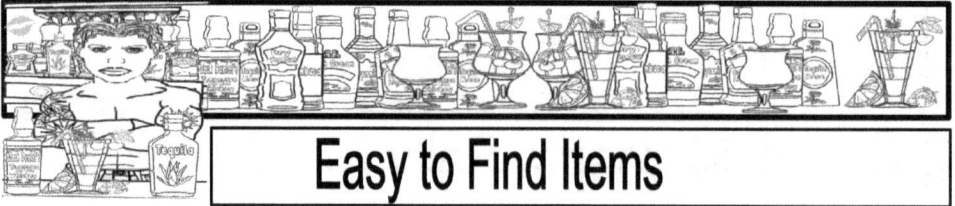

- Fancy Ass Cocktail Glass
- Cocktail Shaker
- 6-10 inch thick Paper Straws
- 1 ounce Shot Glass
- Spear Stir Sticks
- Ice Cubes
- Lime Sour Bar Mix **(*Recipe Page-2*)**
- 69 Cherries LOL (***Just Joking***)
- Fruit for garnish
- Liqueur and Liquor
- Margarita Glass
- Sugar
- Salt

Impaired   Tipsy   Love it!   DD

4

Don't Drink and Drive!
Stop

Plan ahead...Having a Cocktail Party...
or holiday get together?... Do you have
a plan... for getting your guest home...
Safely? ... **Please have a *designated driver***
or provide *Cabs* or *Uber*... for all guests!
Serve food and Non-alcoholic beverages...
provide a spare room for anyone that
might need it! ***Don't drink and Drive... it is***
a Crime!

Impaired   Tipsy   Love it!   DD

Don't
Drink and Drive!
Stop

5

Table of Content

Table of Content

Table of Content

Table of Content

Table of Content

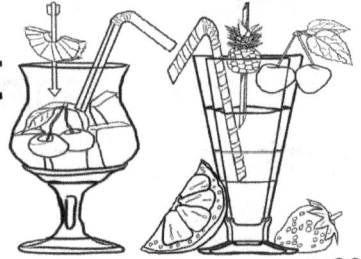

Table of Content

Table of Content

Table of Content

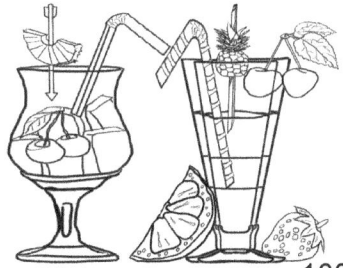

Don't Drink and Drive!
Stop

Rate your Favourite Cocktail or Shot!

Page

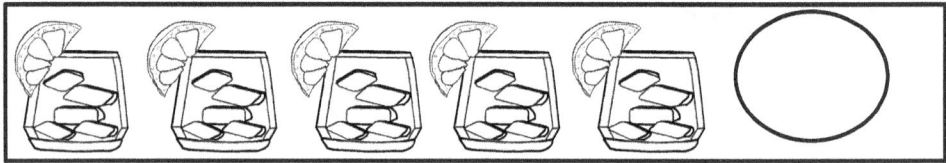

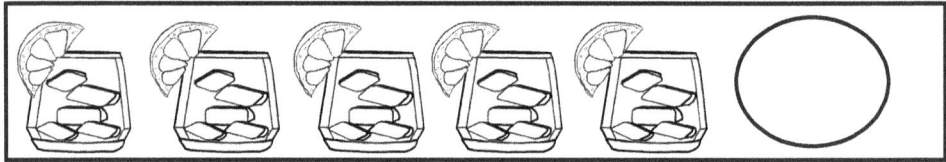

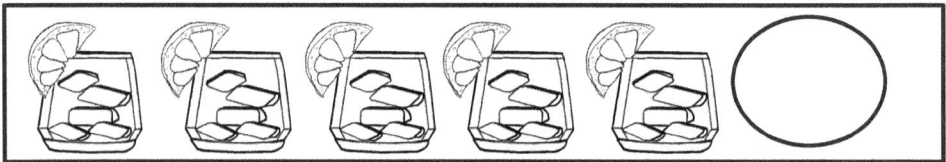

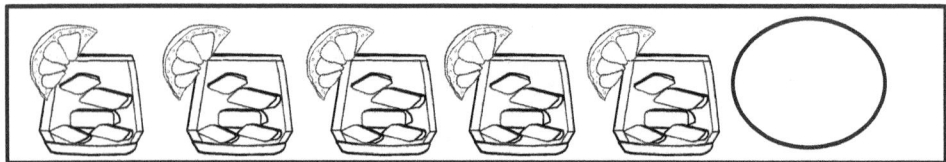

Rate your Favourite Cocktail or Shot!

Page

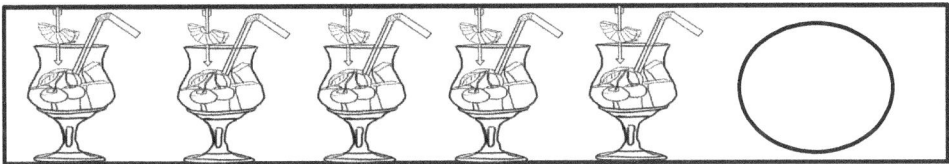

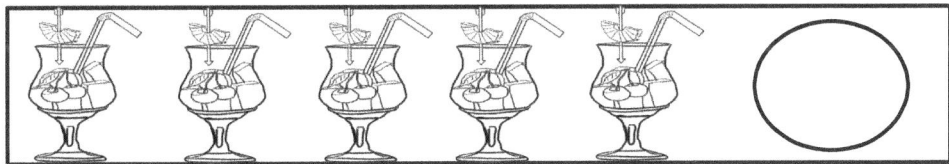

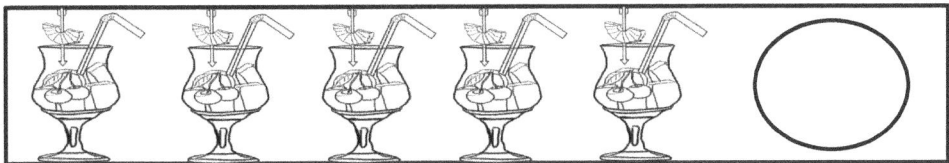

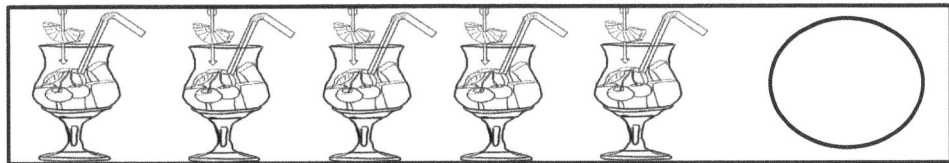

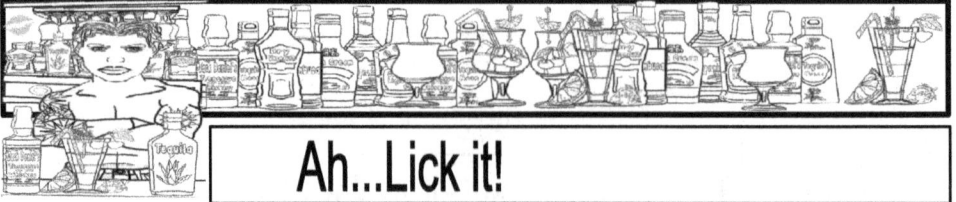

Ah...Lick it!

1 ounce of Coffee Liqueur
1/2 ounce of Irish Creme Liqueur
1/2 ounce of Peppermint Schnapps
Fancy Ass Cocktail Glass
Add Ice Cubes
Top Cocktail Glass with Vanilla flavoured
   Milk or Heavy Cream
Splash of Coca Cola Vanilla Pop
1 Peppermint Candy Stick for Garnish
1 Peppermint Stick finely crushed *(for Rim)*
6-10 in Paper Straw

- Fill your Cocktail Shaker with cold and wet ice cubes...Add your liqueur to Cocktail Shaker... Top with Cream or Flavoured Milk...
- With the Shaker...shake..shake...Wet the rim of *Cocktail Glass and dip into crushed Peppermint stick...*Release liquids from your Cocktail Shaker and pour into your Fancy Cocktail Glass...Add Splash of Vanilla Pop...
- Garnish with Peppermint stick..
- Insert your 6-10 inch Straw...Enjoy!

Impaired   Tipsy   Love it!   DD

Ass & Tits at the Beach

- 1 ounce of Malibu Coconut Rum
- 1 ounce of Amaretto Liqueur
- Fancy Ass Cocktail Glass
- Add Ice Cubes
- Finely Crushed Cherry Candy *(for Rim)*
- Top Cocktail Glass with Orange Juice
- Splash of Grenadine Syrup
- Cherries and Pineapple Wedge for Garnish
- Spear Stir Stick for Garnish
- 6-10 inch Paper Straw

- Fill your Cocktail Shaker with cold and wet ice cubes...Add your Coconut Rum and Amaretto...Top with Orange Juice...Gently shake...***Dip Fancy Cocktail Glass into your crushed Cherry Candy***...Release liquids from your Cocktail Shaker and pour into your Fancy Ass Cocktail Glass...
- Splash of Grenadine Syrup...
- Garnish with Cherries and Pineapple Wedge...
- Insert your 6-10 inch Paper straw... Cheers ..Enjoy!

Don't
Drink and Drive!
Stop

| Impaired | Tipsy | Love it! | DD |

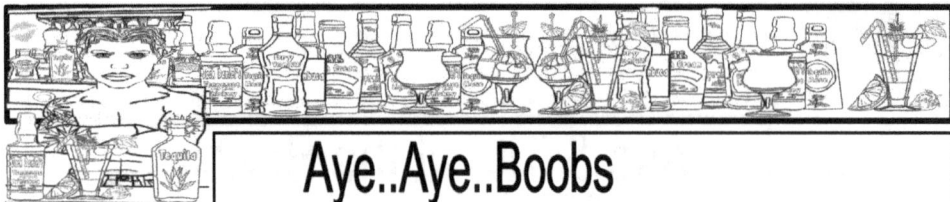

Aye..Aye..Boobs

1 1/2 ounces of Captain Morgan Spiced Rum
Sexy Cocktail Glass
Add Ice Cubes
Top with Ginger Ale
5 Fresh Mint leaves
1/4 of a Mango (Cubes)
1/2 cup Pineapple (cubes)
1 Tsp of Raw Sugar
Mango Slice and Pineapple Wedge
  for garnish
6-10 inch Paper Straw

- Muddle 1/4 of a Mango (cubes) 1/2 cup Pineapple (cubes) ...Mint Leaves...then strain liquids into Cocktail Shaker...Add your Rum... Top with Ginger Ale...Add tsp of Raw Sugar...Holding tight... don't release... slowly....shake...Pour your liquids into Sexy Cocktail Glass...Top with ice cubes (optional)
- Garnish with Mango Wedge and Pineapple Wedge
- Gently insert your 6-10 inch thick Paper Straw... Suck back gently...
  Cheers...Enjoy!

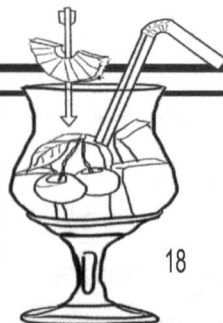

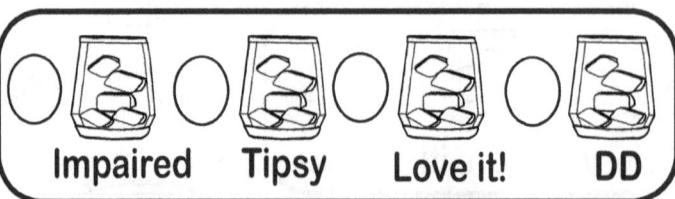

Impaired   Tipsy   Love it!   DD

18

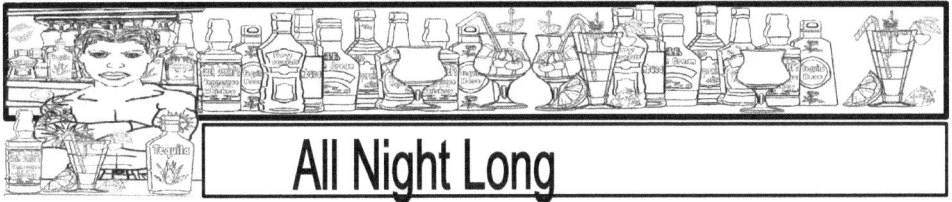

All Night Long

1 ounce of Vodka
Sexy Cocktail Glass
Add Ice Cubes
Splash of Cranberry Juice
Splash of Ginger Ale
Splash of Lime Juice
Can of Red Bull (Energy Drink)
6-10 inch Paper Straw

- Fill your Cocktail Shaker with wet cold
  ice cubes ...Add splash of Cranberry Juice...
  Splash of Ginger Ale...and splash of Lime Juice...
  In rhythmic motion.. shake up and down...
  Grip the rim of Shaker...tight... slowly release
  your sweet liquids into your Sexy Cocktail Glass...
- Top Cocktail Glass with Red Bull...
- Quickly insert your 6-10 inch thick
- straw...Suck back gently ...
  Cheers...Enjoy!

Impaired   Tipsy   Love it!   DD

Don't
Drink and Drive!
Stop

19

Amaretto Sour Sex

1 ounce of Amaretto Liqueur
Fancy Ass Cocktail Glass
Wet and Yes Hard Ice Cubes
1/2 Glass of *Lime Sour Bar Mix (Recipe Page-2)
Top with 7-Up or Sprite
Splash of Grenadine Syrup
6-9 Maraschino Cherries for garnish
Lemon or Citrus Wedges for garnish
Spear Stir Stick for garnish
6-10 inch Paper Straw

- Grab hold of the Cocktail Shaker ..slowly add
  Amaretto Liqueur... 1/2 glass of Lime Sour Bar Mix
- Top with 7-Up (or Sprite)...Do not eject yet
  wait...slowly... shake ...shake...Add your wet cold
  slippery ice cubes ...shake...shake... Grabbing
  the top edge of Shaker...pour slowly...releasing
  liquids into your Fancy Ass Cocktail Glass..Add a
  splash of Grenadine and your Citrus Wedge and
  Cherries for garnish...Quickly insert your
- 6-10 inch thick Paper Straw...
  Cheers...Enjoy!

Impaired   Tipsy   Love it!   DD

A Short Trip to Hell

1 ounce of Jagermeister Liqueur
1/2 ounce of Peach Schnapps
1/2 ounce of Strawberry Schnapps
1/2 ounce of Wild-berry Schnapps
Fancy Ass Cocktail Glass
One Can of Red Bull (Energy Drink)
Wet Ice Cubes *(Heart shaped)*
6-10 inch Paper Straw
One Bitchy or Asshole EX

- Fill your Cocktail Shaker with Heart Shaped ice cubes..slowly... add Jagermeister Liqueur... Peach Schnapps...Strawberry Schnapps... Wild-berry Schnapps....Gently and slowly shake shake...shake....shake...In up and down...motion...
- release...and eject the liquor slowly into your Fancy Cocktail Glass...
- Top with Red Bull ...
- Insert your 6-10 inch Paper Straw... Cheers...Enjoy!

Impaired	Tipsy	Love it!	DD

Don't Drink and Drive! Stop

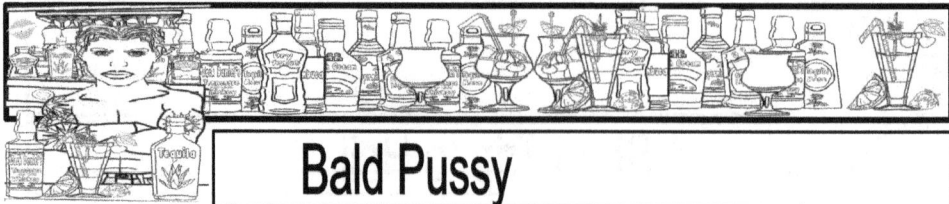

Bald Pussy

- 1 ounce of Vanilla Vodka (Pinnacle)
- 1/2 ounce Melon Liqueur (Bols)
- 1/2 ounce of Silver Tequila
- Fancy Ass Cocktail Glass
- Cold and Wet Ice Cubes
- Top with 7-Up
- Splash of Orange Juice
- 6-9 Ripe Red Cherries for garnish
- Orange Wedge for garnish
- Spear Stir Stick for Cherries
- 6-10 inch Paper Straw

- Fill Cocktail Shaker with your Vanilla Vodka...
  Melon Liqueur... Silver Tequila...and slowly
  add your hard ice cubes...Top with 7-Up...
- Grabbing the top edge of Shaker..grip tightly...
  pouring slowly... releasing liquids into your Fancy
  Ass Cocktail Glass... Add splash of Orange Juice
- Garnish with 6-9 Cherries...and Orange wedge...
- Quickly insert your large Pink 6-10 inch
  thick straw...
  Cheers...Enjoy!

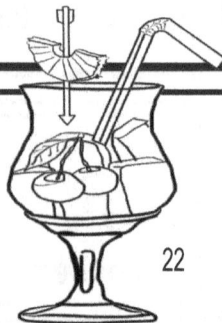

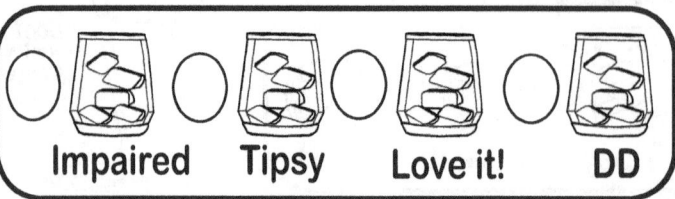

Impaired   Tipsy   Love it!   DD

22

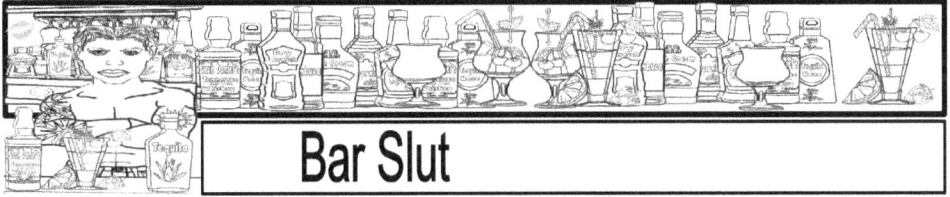

Bar Slut

- 1 ounce of Vodka
- 1/2 ounce of Grapefruit Vodka(Absolut)
- 1/2 ounce of Sour Puss Lemon Liqueur
- Sexy Cocktail Glass
- Add Ice Cubes
- Top with Ginger Ale or Sprite
- Splash of Lime Sour Mix *(Recipe page-2)*
- 6-9 Ripe Red Cherries for garnish
- Lemon Wedge for garnish
- Spear Stir Stick for garnish
- 6-10 inch Paper Straw

- Fill Cocktail Shaker with Vodka...Sour Puss...
- Add your ice cubes...Top with Ginger Ale... Shake shake...shake...
- Grabbing the top edge of Shaker..grip tightly... pour slowly... releasing into your Sexy Ass Cocktail Glass...Splash of Lime Sour Bar Mix...
- Garnish with 6-9 Cherries and Lemon Wedge
- Quickly insert your large Black 6-10 inch Thick straw... Cheers...Enjoy!

| Impaired | Tipsy | Love it! | DD |

Don't
Drink and Drive!
Stop

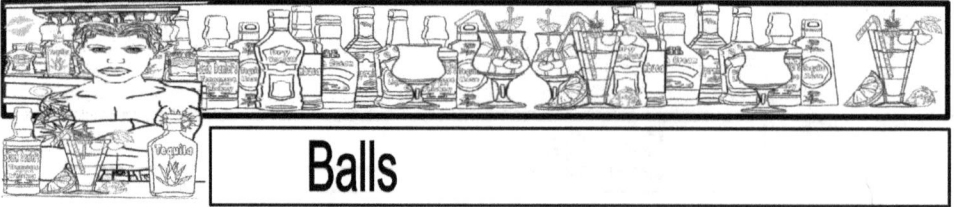

Balls

- 1/2 ounce of Coffee Liqueur
- 1/2 ounce of Yukon Jack
- Shot Glass
  Cheers...Enjoy!

Beamers

- 1/2 ounce of Jim Beam Bourbon Whiskey
- 1/2 ounce of Budweiser Lager
- Shot Glass
  Cheers...Enjoy!

For Women:<u>when he asks to get into your pants,</u> just say, No thanks, I have one Asshole in there already.

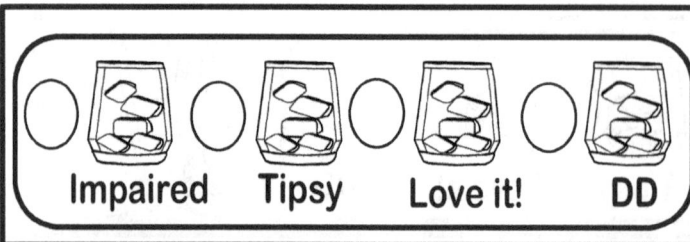

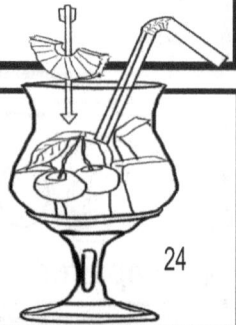

24

Bee's Buzz

- 1 ounce of Dillon's Rose Gin (any flavoured Gin)
- 1/2 ounce of Spiced Honey Liqueur (Krupnik)
- Margarita Glass *(Wet Margarita Rim)*
- **Margarita Rim (Salted Rim Recipe Page-3)**
- Add Ice Cubes
- Top with Sprite or Ginger Ale
- 1/2 ounce of Lemon Juice
- 2 Cherries for Garnish or Lemon Slice(twist)
- Spear Stir Stick for Garnish
- 6-10 inch Yellow Paper Straw

- Fill Cocktail Shaker with wet ice cubes...
- Add your Gin and Honey Liqueur to the Cocktail Shaker...Top with Sprite...Gently shake... in a up and down motion... shake your liquids....shake...**Dip your Margarita Rim into the Salty Margarita Mixture *(Recipe Page-3)***
- Eject your liquids into coated rim Margarita Glass..
- Garnish with Lemon twist and Cherries...
- Quickly insert your Yellow 6-10 inch straw... Cheers...Enjoy!

Impaired   Tipsy   Love it!   DD

Don't Drink and Drive **Stop**

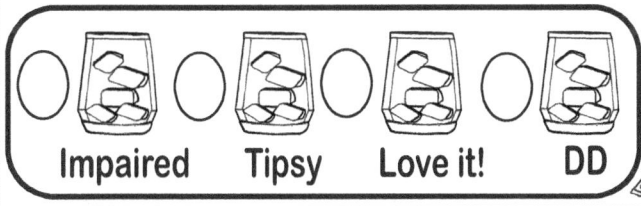

25

Bed Head

1/2 ounce of Sambuca Liqueur
1/2 ounce of Tequila Rose Liqueur
Shot Glass
Cheers...Enjoy!

Will you sleep with me tonight?
Cuz I'm afraid of the dark!

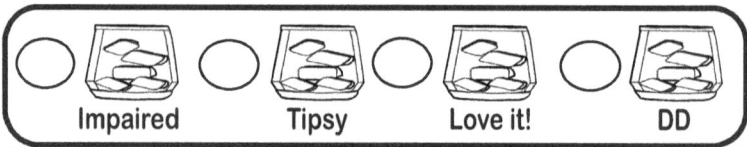

Impaired	Tipsy	Love it!	DD
○	○	○	○

Beg...You Salty Dog

1 ounce of Lemon Gin
1 ounce Lemon Vodka (Absolut)
Fancy Ass Cocktail Glass (Wet Rim)
2 tbsp of Pink Salt for rim of Glass
Dip Cocktail Glass rim into plate of salt
Top with Ginger Ale or Sprite
Splash of Grapefruit Juice
1 Grapefruit Slice for Garnish
6-10 inch Paper Straw
Cheers...Enjoy!

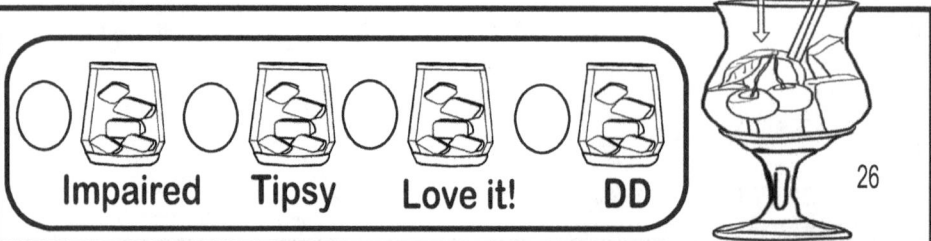

Impaired	Tipsy	Love it!	DD
○	○	○	○

26

Bedroom Wet Sheets

- 1 ounce of Malibu Coconut Rum
- 1/4 ounce of Peach Schnapps
- 1/2 ounce of Vodka
- 1/4 ounce of Amaretto Liqueur
- Sexy Cocktail Glass
- Add Ice Cubes
- Top with Orange Juice
- 6-9 Cherries for garnish
- Spear Stir Stick
- 6-10 inch Paper Straw

- Grabbing hold of Cocktail Shaker ...add Malibu Rum...Schnapps...Vodka...Amaretto...
- Do not eject yet...top with Orange Juice
- Wait...wait..slowly ...fill with wet cold slippery cubes ...shake...hold tightly... Grabbing the top edge... pour liquids slowly... releasing into your Sexy Cocktail Glass...Strain if you wish...
- Garnish with your 6-9 Cherries ...
- Quickly insert your 6-10 inch thick Paper straw...Cheers...Enjoy!

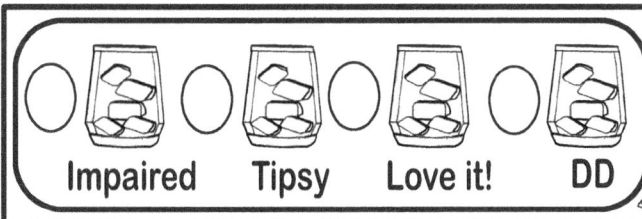

Impaired   Tipsy   Love it!   DD

Don't Drink and Drive! **Stop**

27

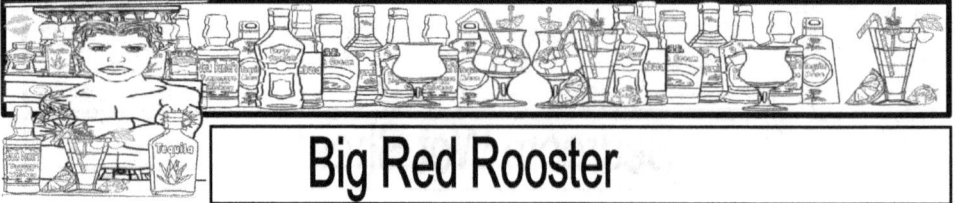

Big Red Rooster

1/2 ounce of Tequila Coconut (1800)
1/2 ounce of Amaretto Liqueur
Chilled Fancy and Sexy Cocktail Glass
Add Ice Cubes
Top with Pineapple Juice
Splash of Grenadine Syrup
Pineapple Wedge for garnish
6-9 Sweet Cherries for garnish
Spear Stir Stick
6-10 inch Colourful Straw

- In a Cocktail Shaker...add Tequila and Amaretto Liqueur...Top with Pineapple Juice...Add a splash of Grenadine......Shake up and down...
- Pour into your Fancy Cocktail Glass...
- Add Pineapple Wedge and Cherries on Spear Stir Stick for garnish....
- Quickly insert your large 6-10 inch thick Paper straw...
  Cheers...Enjoy!

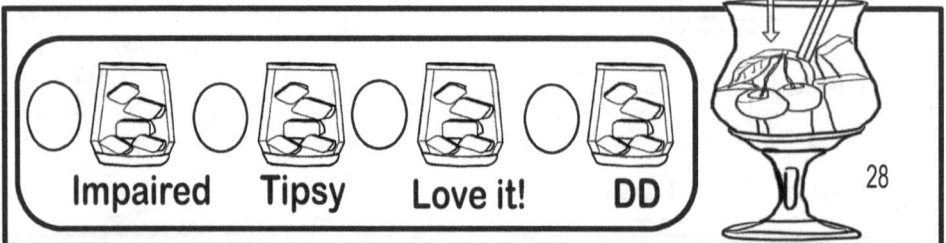

Impaired   Tipsy   Love it!   DD

28

Blood Red Margaritas

1 ounce of Orange Tequila (Agavero Orange)
1/2 ounce of Grand Mariner Liqueur
Chilled Margarita Glass *(Wet Glass Rim)*
Add Ice Cubes
1 1/2 ounces of Simple Syrup *(Recipe Page-2)*
1 ounce of Fresh Lime Juice
Top Margarita Glass with Orange Juice
Salt the Rim *(Margarita Salt Recipe Page - 3)*
Lime and Blood Red Orange Wedge for garnish

- With your fingers.... run your Lime Wedge around the Rim of your Margarita Glass...take your time..
- Dip Margarita Glass into salty mixture... set aside...
- Combine your Orange Tequila...Grand Mariner Liqueur and all other liquids into Shaker with cold wet ice cubes...Shake for 30 seconds... Strain...into your *(salted-rimmed)* Margarita glass
- Garnish with a twist or slice of Orange and Lime...
- Repeat to make more Cocktails Cheers...Enjoy!

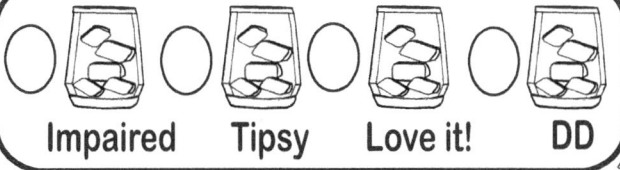

Impaired   Tipsy   Love it!   DD

Don't Drink and Drive! **Stop**

29

Best Friend Rocks

- 1/2 ounce of Blue Raspberry Lemonade
- Vodka *(Smirnoff)*
- 1/2 ounce of Blue Curacao Liqueur
- Shot Glass *(Wet Rim)*
- Finely Crushed Blue Pop Rocks Candy
  (Dip Rim of the Shot Glass into Pop Rocks)
- Splash of Lime Juice
- Cheers.......Enjoy

Impaired	Tipsy	Love it!	DD

Big Balls..Lick my Panda

- 1/2 ounce of Vodka
- 1/2 ounce of Tequila Rose Liqueur
- Shot Glass
  Cheers...Enjoy!

No Glove, No Love!

Impaired	Tipsy	Love it!	DD

30

Big Sunset Banger

1 ounce of Vodka
1/2 ounce of Peach Schnapps Liqueur
Fancy Ass Cocktail Glass
Add Ice Cubes
Top glass with Lemonade
Splash of Orange Juice
Splash of Cranberry Juice
Splash of Grenadine Syrup
Cherries and Pineapple Wedge for garnish
Spear Stir Stick for garnish
6-10 inch Paper Straw

- Fill your Cocktail Shaker with wet ice cubes
- Add Vodka and Peach Schnapps...Top with Lemonade and splash of Cranberry and Orange Juice...Splash of Grenadine...Gently and slowly... shake... in up and down motion...
- Eject the liquids slowly into your Fancy Cocktail Glass...Garnish with Cherries and Pineapple Wedge
- Quickly insert your 6-10 inch Paper Straw... Cheers..... Enjoy!

Impaired   Tipsy   Love it!   DD

Don't Drink and Drive! Stop

31

Blue Balls Mojito

1 ounce of Rum
Fancy Ass Cocktail Glass
Add Ice Cubes
1 Kiwi Peeled
1/4 cup of Blueberries
1 Teaspoon of Raw Sugar
Top Glass with Soda
Spear Stir Stick for Garnish
Passion Fruit for Garnish
6-10 inch Paper Straw

- Muddle 1/4 cup of Blueberries and Kiwi then strain into the Cocktail Shaker...
- Add the Raw Sugar or any sweetener...
- Add your Rum and top with Soda...
- Fill the Shaker with ice... grip tight... don't release...slowly...slowly...shake and strain... into your Fancy Sexy Glass...
- Garnish with Passion fruit...
- Gently insert your 6-10 inch thick Straw... Suck back... Cheers...Enjoy!

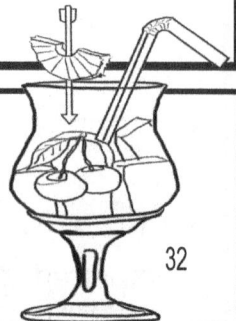

Impaired   Tipsy   Love it!   DD

Blow My Load

- 1/4 ounce of Jack Daniels Whiskey
- 1/4 ounce of Johnnie Walker
- 1/4 ounce of Jim Beam Bourbon
- 1/4 ounce of Gold Tequila
- Fancy Cocktail Glass
- Stiff ounce of Sour Lime Bar-mix *(Recipe Page-2)*
- Top Cocktail Glass with Sprite or Ginger Ale
- Three Red Ripe Cherries
- Banana for Garnish and 3 more Cherries
- Spear Stir Stick for Garnish
- 6-10 inch Paper Straw

- Fill your Cocktail Shaker with all your liquids...
- Add wet cold ice cubes... In rhythmic motion.. shake...grip the rim tight...strain and release liquids from Cocktail Shaker...
- Wait......wait......slowly.... eject into Fancy Ass Cocktail Glass...
- Garnish with Cherries and big Banana slice... on a Spear Stir Stick
- Drop your 3 Sweet Cherries into Cocktail Glass
- Quickly insert your 6-10 inch (paper) thick Straw Suck back gently and Enjoy!

Impaired   Tipsy   Love it!   DD

Don't
Drink and Drive
Stop

33

Blow Job

- 1/2 ounce of Bailey's Irish Cream
- 1/2 ounce of Amaretto Liqueur
- Shot Glass
- Cherry for Garnish
- **Top Shot Glass with Whipped Cream**
- Cherry on top of Whipped Cream
  Cheers...Enjoy!

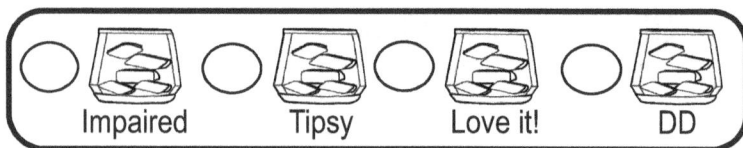

Impaired	Tipsy	Love it!	DD

Big... Big... Bulge

- 1/3 ounce of Black Sambuca Liqueur
- 1/3 ounce of Tequila Rose Liqueur
- 1/3 ounce of Blue Curacao Liqueur
- Shot Glass
- **Top Shot Glass with Whipped Cream**
  Cheers...Enjoy!

Impaired	Tipsy	Love it!	DD

Big... Big... Lick!

- 1/3 ounce of Vodka
- 1/3 ounce of Southern Comfort
- 1/3 ounce of Grand Marnier Liqueur
- Shot Glass *(Wet Rim)*
- Finely Crushed Cherry Lollipop Candy
- *Dip Shot Glass into Crushed Cherry Candy*
- *Top Liquor filled Shot Glass with Whipped Cream*
- Cheers...Enjoy!

- Gently run your fingers... slowly around the rim of your Shot Glass... When ready... wet rim...with Grenadine Syrup...
- Dip Shot Glass into crushed Cherry Candy stick...
- Slowly...add your liquor....to your shot glass....
- Grabbing hold of the Whipped Cream spout... pull back.. and slowly release...spraying all over the top of the shot glass...
  Cheers...Enjoy!

Impaired   Tipsy   Love it!   DD

Don't Drink and Drive! **Stop**

35

Brown Painted Horse

1/2 ounce of Chocolate Creme Liqueur
1/2 ounce of Dooley's Toffee Vodka
1/2 ounce of Yukon Jack Liqueur
Sexy Cocktail Glass
Add Ice Cubes
Top Glass with Sprite
Peppermint Leaves (*Sprig*)
1 Granny Smith Apple Sliced for Garnish
Chocolate Syrup (*Magic Shell*)
6-10 inch Paper Straw
Spear Stir Stick

- Muddle your Mint Leaves in a Cocktail Shaker...
- Slowly add all liquids... grip tightly... don't release...
- Holding firmly to the Cocktail Shaker... shake... strain...and release your liquids into Sexy Glass ...Add your ice cubes...
- Dip Granny Smith Apple Slices into Magic Shell Chocolate... for garnish...
- insert your 6-10 inch Brown Paper Straw...Suck back gently...
  Cheers ...Enjoy!

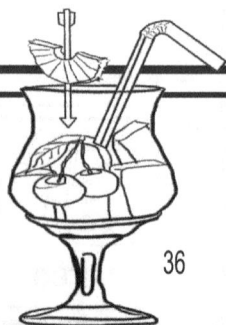

Impaired   Tipsy   Love it!   DD

36

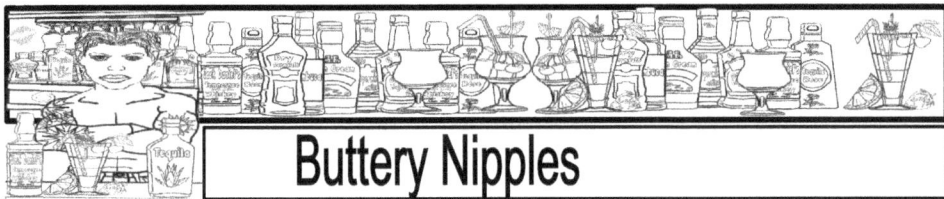

Buttery Nipples

1/2 ounce of Butterscotch Liqueur
1/2 ounce of Bailey's Irish Cream
Shot Glass
Butterscotch Syrup *(Dip Rim of Shot Glass)*
Finely Crushed Werther's Original Candy
Whipped Cream for top of Shot Glass
   Cheers...Enjoy!

- With your fingers... slowly wet the rim of your shot glass.. when ready...
- Dip Shot Glass into Butterscotch Syrup...
- Dip into finely crushed Werther's Original candy... Slowly...add your liquor...to your Shot Glass....
- Gently grab hold of the Whipped Cream spout... pull back.. and slowly release...spray all the the top of the Shot Glass...
Cheers... Enjoy!

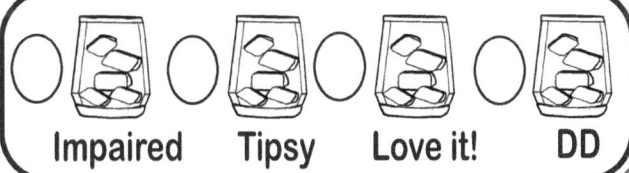

Impaired   Tipsy   Love it!   DD

Don't Drink and Drive Stop

Blackberry Lipstick

1 1/2 ounces of Blackberry Gin
Sexy Shaped Cocktail Glass
Add Iced Cubes
1/4 cup of Simple Syrup **(Page-2 recipe)**
Top Cocktail Glass with Tonic Water
Blue Edible Glitter Spray (***Food Grade***)
12 Blackberries
Sprig of fresh Mint Leaves
Splash of Lemon Juice
Spear Stir Stick
Fancy 6-10 inch Paper Straw

- Spray your Sexy Glass with edible Black or Blue Glitter Spray (***Optional)***
- Muddle your Blackberries and Mint Leaves and strain...into Shaker...Add Simple Syrup and splash of Lemon Juice...shake ...shake...
- Add your Blackberry Gin and top your Glass with Tonic Water and add ice cubes and stir...Garnish
- with some Mint Leaves and Lemon slice or twist Quickly insert your 6-10 inch straw... Cheers and Enjoy!

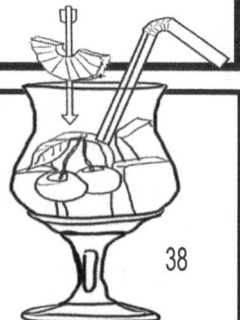

Impaired   Tipsy   Love it!   DD

38

Bite Me

- 1/2 ounce of Malibu Rum
- 1/2 ounce of Jagermeister Liqueur
- Shot Glass
  Cheers...Enjoy!

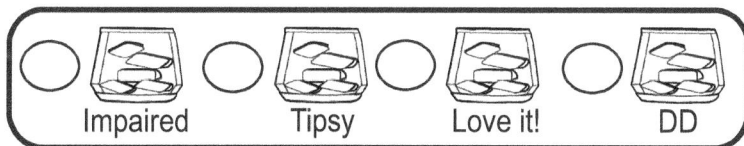

◯ Impaired ◯ Tipsy ◯ Love it! ◯ DD

Bye For Now!

- 1/3 ounce of Tequila Rose Liqueur
- 1/3 ounce of Tequila Java Liqueur
- 1/3 ounce of Tequila Cocoa Liqueur
- Shot Glass
  Cheers... Enjoy!

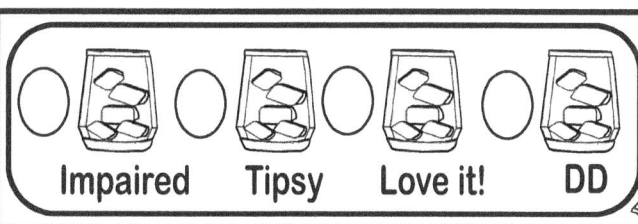

◯ Impaired ◯ Tipsy ◯ Love it! ◯ DD

Don't Drink and Drive! **Stop**

Cherry Pop

1 ounce of Jack Daniels
1/2 ounce of Amaretto Liqueur
1/2 ounce of Ginger Brandy
Sexy Ass Cocktail Glass
1 can of Cherry Cola
Splash of Tonic Water or Ginger Ale
6-9 Cherries or Cherry Juice
Orange Wedge and 2 Cherries
for Garnish
Spear Stir Stick for Garnish
6-10 inch Paper Straw

- Muddle Cherries in a Cocktail Shaker...
- Muddle until smashed... Add your
  Spirits..strain into Cocktail Glass....
- Add your ice cubes..Top with Cherry
  Cola and a Splash of Tonic Water
- Garnish with 2 Cherries and Orange
  Wedge... with a Spear Stir Stick...
- Add additional Cherries if you like them
  to burst them into your mouth!
  Cheers...Enjoy!

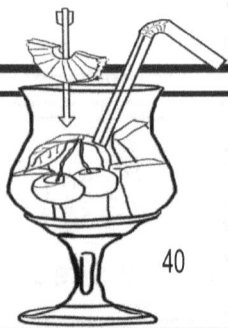

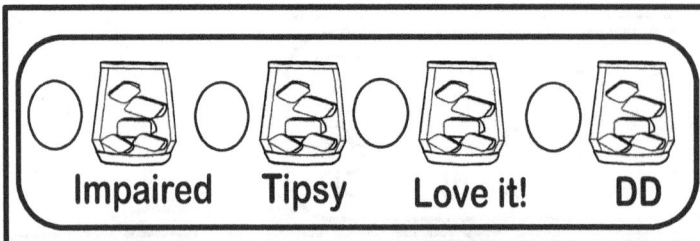

Impaired   Tipsy   Love it!   DD

40

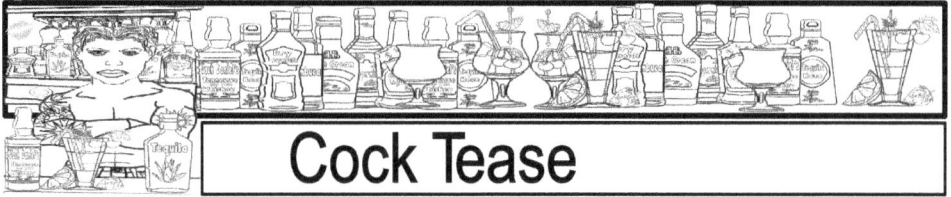

Cock Tease

1/2 ounce of Creme de Menthe Liqueur
1/2 ounce of Peppermint Schnapps
Shot Glass
Splash of Grenadine Syrup
Layer these liqueurs as listed...
red...green...white
Cheers...Enjoy!

Impaired	Tipsy	Love it!	DD
○	○	○	○

Correct... is it Raining Purple

1 ounce of Blue Curacao Liqueur
1/2 ounce of Vodka
Fancy Ass Cocktail Glass
Add Ice Cubes
Top with Pineapple Juice
Splash of Apple Juice
Splash of Grenadine Syrup
6-10 Paper Blue Straw
Cheers...Enjoy!

Don't Drink and Drive! **Stop**

Impaired	Tipsy	Love it!	DD
○	○	○	○

41

Caught You..Cheater

- 1/2 ounce of Amaretto Liqueur
- 1/2 ounce of Canadian Club Whiskey
- Shot Glass *(Wet Rim)*
- 2 Tbsp of Pink Salt Sprinkled on Plate
- *Dip rim of shot glass into the Pink Salt*
- Fill shot glass with your Liquor
- One Sour Lemon Wedge to Suck On
  Cheers...Enjoy!

Impaired	Tipsy	Love it!	DD

Call Me

- 1/2 ounce of Amaretto Liqueur
- 1/2 ounce of Jagermeister Liqueur
- Shot Glass *(Wet Rim)*
- 2 Tbsp of Sugar sprinkled on plate to coat Shot Glass rim
- *Dip rim of the shot glass into the Sugar*
- Fill shot glass with your Liquor
- Splash of Pineapple Juice
  Cheers...Enjoy!

Impaired	Tipsy	Love it!	DD

42

Citrus Pimp

1 ounce of Melon Liqueur
1/2 ounce of White Creme De Cacao
Liqueur
Fancy Cocktail Glass
Add Ice Cubes
Top with Sprite
Splash of Cranberry Juice
Garnish with a Pineapple Slice
Spear Stir Stick
6-10 inch Paper Straw

- Fill your Cocktail Shaker with all your liquor...
- Add wet cold ice cubes...top with Sprite... In a rhythmic motion.. shake...Grip the rim tight... strain and release liquid from Cocktail Shaker...
- Wait......wait......slowly.... eject into your Fancy Ass Cocktail Glass..**_Top with more Sprite if needed_**...Splash of Cranberry Juice...
- Garnish with Pineapple slice on a Spear Stir Stick
- Quickly insert your 6-10 inch (paper) thick Straw Suck back gently and Enjoy!

Impaired   Tipsy   Love it!   DD

Don't
Drink and Drive!
Stop

43

Captain's Booty

- 1 ounce of Captain Morgan Spiced Rum
- 1/2 ounce of Coconut Tequila
- Fancy Ass Cocktail Glass
- Crushed Ice Cubes
- Top with Ginger Ale Pop
- Splash of Grenadine Syrup
- Garnish with Pineapple Slice
- Spear Stir Stick
- 6-10 inch Black Straw

- Fill your Cocktail Shaker with Rum...Tequila and top with Ginger Ale...
- Add wet cold ice cubes... In rhythmic motion.. shake..Grip the shaker rim tight...
- Release liquid from Cocktail Shaker...Wait......wait slowly...eject into Fancy Ass Cocktail Glass...
- Splash of Grenadine Syrup...
- Garnish with Pineapple slice on a Spear Stir Stick...
- Quickly insert your 6-10 inch (paper) thick Straw... Suck back gently and Enjoy!

Impaired   Tipsy   Love it!   DD

44

Captain with a Skirt

- 2 ounces of White Wine
- 1/2 ounce of Captain Morgan Spiced Rum
- Fancy Ass Cocktail Glass
- Cold Ice Cubes
- Top Glass with Coca-Cola or Diet
- 1 Slice of Lime Garnish
- 3 Cherries for Garnish
- Spear Stir Stick for Garnish
- 6-10 inch Paper Straw

- Fill your Cocktail Shaker with Wine and Rum
- Top Cocktail Glass with Coca-Cola or Diet Cola...
- Add wet cold ice cubes... In rhythmic motion... shake..Grip the rim tight...holding.. and release liquid from Cocktail Shaker... Wait...wait...slowly.... eject into Fancy Ass Cocktail Glass...
- Garnish with slice of Lime and 3 Cherries on a Spear Stir Stick...
- Quickly insert your 6-10 inch thick Straw... Suck back gently and Enjoy!

| Impaired | Tipsy | Love it! | DD |

Don't
Drink and Drive
Stop

45

Cherry Popper

1 ounce of Cherry Schnapps
1/2 ounce of Cherry Brandy Liqueur
Fancy Ass Cocktail Glass
Add Ice Cubes
Top Cocktail Glass with Ginger Ale
6-9 Cherries
Spear Stir stick for Cherries
6-10 inch Red Paper Straw
Cheers...Enjoy!

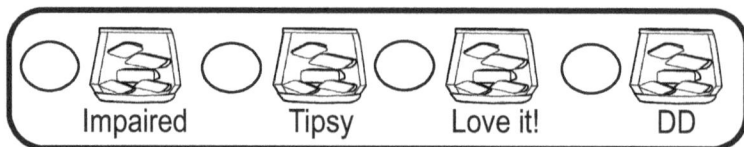

Impaired   Tipsy   Love it!   DD

Chase Me

1/3 ounce of Amaretto Liqueur
1/3 ounce of Wild Berry Schnapps
1/3 ounce of Doctor Pepper
Shot Glass
Cheers...Enjoy!

1 Set of Car Keys...and
Hot Electric Car

Impaired   Tipsy   Love it!   DD

46

Chocolate Fuzzy

- 1/2 ounce of Vodka
- 1/2 ounce of Frangelico (Hazel Nut) Liqueur
- Shot Glass
- Spray some Whipped Cream *(on top of Shot Glass)*
- Drizzle of Dark Chocolate Syrup on Whipped Cream head

  Cheers...Enjoy!

◯ Impaired ◯ Tipsy ◯ Love it! ◯ DD

Crazy Vodka Buzz

- 1/3 ounce of Pink Lemonade Vodka (New Amsterdam)
- 1/3 ounce of Passionfruit Vodka (New Amsterdam)
- 1/3 ounce of Vanilla Vodka (Pinnacle)
- Shot Glass

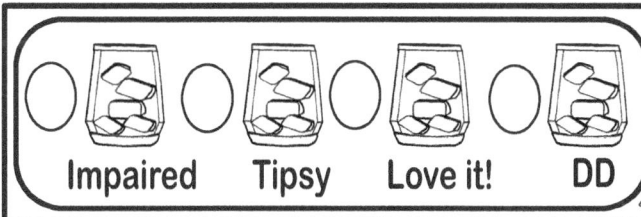

  Cheers...Enjoy!

◯ Impaired ◯ Tipsy ◯ Love it! ◯ DD

Don't Drink and Drive **Stop**

47

Dick Head

1/3 ounce of Amaretto Liqueur
1/3 ounce of Sloe Gin Liqueur
1/3 ounce of of Cranberry Juice
Shot Glass
  Cheers...Enjoy!

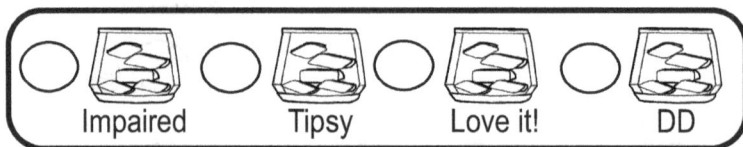

Impaired		Tipsy		Love it!		DD
○		○		○		

Dick Me

1/2 ounce of Butterscotch Schnapps
1/2 ounce of Captain Morgan Spiced Rum
Shot Glass
  Cheers...Enjoy!

Impaired	Tipsy	Love it!	DD

48

Dildo

1/4 ounce of Vodka
1/4 ounce of Raspberry Liqueur
1/4 ounce of Lime Bar Mix
1/4 ounce of Silver Tequila
Shot Glass
Cheers...Enjoy!

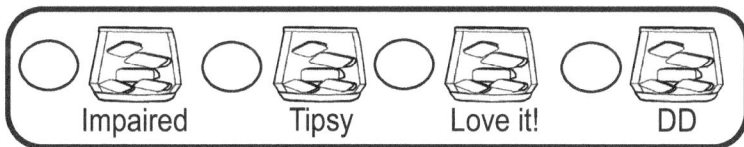

○ Impaired   ○ Tipsy   ○ Love it!   ○ DD

Do Me Please!

1/4 ounce of Cola Pop
1/4 ounce of Amaretto Liqueur
1/4 ounce of Silver Tequila
1/4 ounce of Southern Comfort
Shot Glass
Cheers...Enjoy!

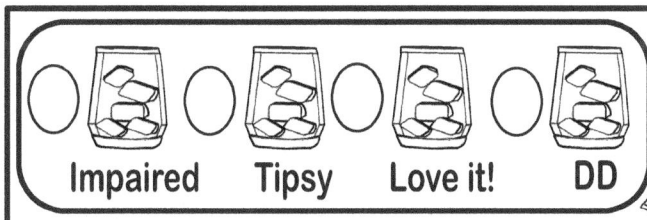

○ Impaired   ○ Tipsy   ○ Love it!   ○ DD

Don't Drink and Drive Stop

49

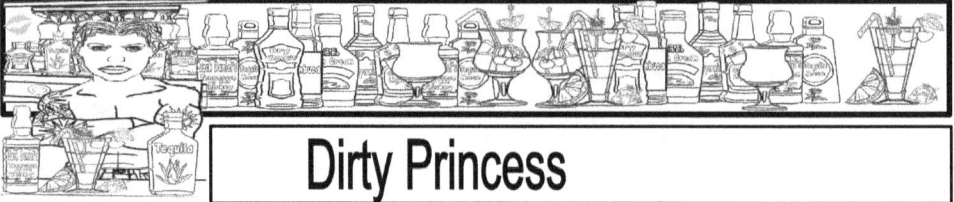

Dirty Princess

1 ounce of Bailey's Irish Cream Liqueur
1/2 ounce of Vodka
1/2 ounce of White Creme de Menthe Liqueur
1/2 ounce of Kahlua Liqueur
Sexy Princess Cocktail Glass
Add Ice Cubes
Top with Heavy Cream or Vanilla Flavoured Milk
Chocolate Shell
Strawberries *dipped in Chocolate Shell*
Spear Stir Stick for Chocolate Strawberries
6-10 inch Pink Paper Straw

- Fill your Cocktail Shaker with your Irish Cream and Vodka...Kahlua...Creme de Menthe Liqueur and...Flavoured Milk or Heavy Cream...
- Add wet cold ice cubes... In rhythmic motion... shake...Grip the rim tight...holding.. release liquid from Cocktail Shaker...into the Sexy Cocktail Glass..Dip Strawberries into Chocolate Shell...and garnish glass
- Quickly insert your 6-10 inch Pink (paper) thick Straw... Suck back gently and Enjoy!

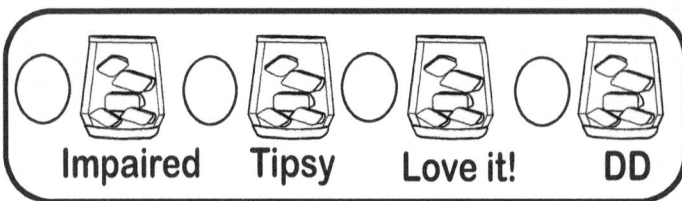

Impaired   Tipsy   Love it!   DD

50

Eat Me!

1/2 ounce of Frangelico Liqueur
1/2 ounce of Peppermint Schnapps
Shot Glass *(Wet the Rim)*
Shot Glass dipped in Finely Crushed Strawberry Candy
Cheers...Enjoy!
1 Ice Cube for Lubrication

Impaired	Tipsy	Love it!	DD

Exit... My Sour Puss

1/3 ounce of Sour Puss Watermelon Liqueur
1/3 ounce of Sour Puss Tangerine Liqueur
1/3 ounce of Sour Puss Pina Colada Liqueur
Shot Glass
Cheers...Enjoy!

Impaired	Tipsy	Love it!	DD

Don't Drink and Drive! **Stop**

51

Energy Blaster

- 1 ounce of Vanilla Vodka (Faber)
- 1 ounce of Amaretto Liqueur
- 1 Hell of a Fancy Ass Cocktail Glass
- 1 Can of Red Bull (Energy Drink)
- *1 Espresso filled Shot Glass*
- Drop your *Vodka Filled Shot Glass* into Red Bull filled Fancy Ass Cocktail Glass
- Chase with your Espresso Shot

1.....2....3... Lift OFF

Blast Off!   Blast Off!   Blast Off!

- Fill your Cocktail Shaker with wet cold ice cubes...
- Add your Amaretto Liqueur... top with Red Bull...
- In rhythmic motion shake..Grip the rim of Shaker tight...holding..slowly release liquid from Cocktail Shaker into your Sexy Ass Glass....
- Drop your *Vanilla Vodka Filled Shot Glass* into Red Bull filled Sexy Ass Cocktail Glass...
- Chase with your Espresso filled shot glass Suck back gently and Enjoy!

Impaired   Tipsy   Love it!   DD

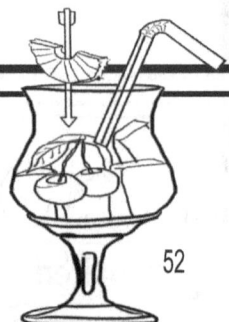

52

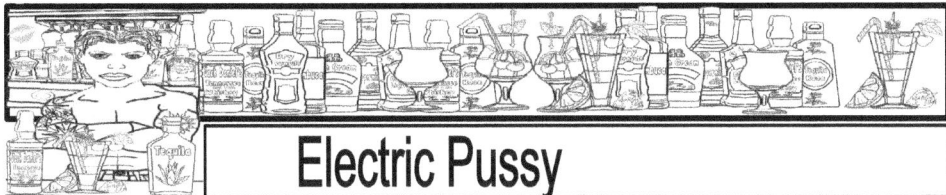

Electric Pussy

1/2 ounce of Silver Tequila

1/2 ounce of Raspberry Sour Puss Liqueur

2 Shot Glasses

1 ounce of Lemon Gin *(in Shot Glass)*

Fancy Cocktail Glass *(Sugar and Salt Rimmed)*

2Tbsp of Sugar and Pinch of Salt

(Cocktail Glass Rim)

1 Can of Red Bull (Energy Drink)

**Drop your Tequila...Raspberry Sour Puss
Shot Glass into your Red Bull filled Cocktail Glass**

- Dip your Fancy Cocktail Glass rim into Sugar and Salt mixture (2 tbsp sugar and pinch salt)
- Fill Cocktail Glass with your Red Bull
- Fill shot glass with Tequila and Sour Puss Liqueur
- Then gently drop your Tequila and Raspberry Liqueur shot into your Fancy Glass... filled with your can of Red Bull...
- *Separately in the other shot glass fill with 1 ounce of Lemon Gin....*
  Cheers...Enjoy!

Impaired   Tipsy   Love it!   DD

Don't
Drink and Drive!
Stop

53

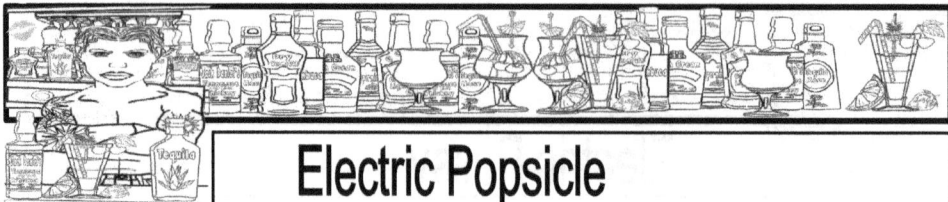

Electric Popsicle

- 1 ounce of Melon Liqueur
- 1/2 ounce of Blue Curacao Liqueur
- Top with Lime Sour Bar Mix
- 1 ~~Fucking~~ Large Fancy Cocktail Glass
- Add Ice Cubes
- Splash of Sprite
- Watermelon Slice and 6-9 Cherries for garnish
- Spear Stir Stick for garnish
- 6-10 inch Blue Paper Straw
  Cheers...Enjoy!

Homemade Lime Sour Bar Mix
- 1 Cup of Sugar
- 1 Cup of Water
- 1/2 Cup of freshly squeezed Lemon
- 1/2 Cup of freshly squeezed Lime
- Heat Liquids on stove to dissolve Sugar
- Let Cool

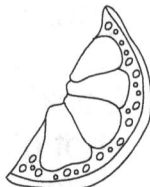

Optional; add 2 egg whites Whipped to Sour Mix to make Cocktail Slightly Foamy

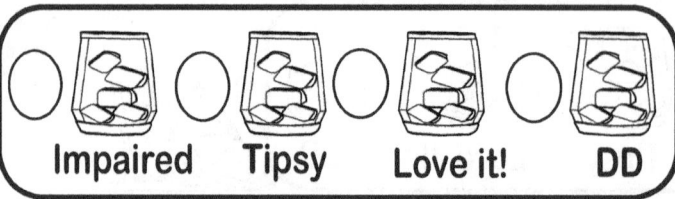

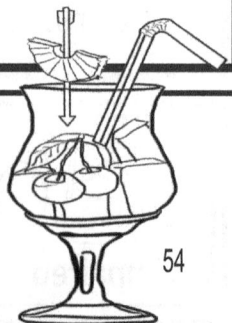

Impaired   Tipsy   Love it!   DD

54

End of the Road

1 ounce of Frangelico Liqueur
1 ounce of Cherry Whiskey
Fancy Ass Cocktail Glass
Add Ice Cubes
Top Cocktail Glass with Heavy Cream or Milk
4 Pumps of Whipped Cream (**for *top of Cocktail Glass*)**
Cherries for garnish and Spear Stir Stick
6-10 inch Paper Straw
3 Nuts or Friends (Lol....Just Kidding)

- Grabbing hold of Cocktail Shaker ...add Frangelico and Cherry Whiskey...Do not eject yet...add your Heavy Cream... Wait slowly in a rhythmic motion... shake..add wet cold slippery cubes ...shake...
- Grabbing the top edge of the Shaker... pour slowly releasing into your Cocktail Glass..
- Top with your Whipped Cream...and Cherries for garnish...
- Insert your 6-10 inch Paper Straw... Cheers...Enjoy!

Don't
Drink and Drive!
Stop

Impaired   Tipsy   Love it!   DD

55

1/2 ounce of Melon Liqueur
1/2 ounce of Butterscotch Schnapps
1 ounce of Chocolate Vodka (360)
2 Shot Glasses
Fancy Ass Cocktail Glass
Can of Red Bull (any energy drink)

Bottoms Up!

- Fill shot glass with Melon Liqueur and Butterscotch Liqueur...set aside...
- In your Cocktail Glass fill with can of Red Bull...gently drop your **Melon Liqueur and Butterscotch liqueur filled shot glass** into your Red Bull filled Fancy Ass Cocktail Glass ...
- **Chase with 1 ounce shot of Chocolate Vodka** Cheers...Enjoy!

Impaired   Tipsy   Love it!   DD

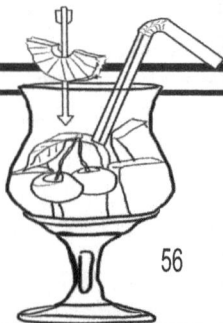

56

Face Fuck

1/4 ounce of Amaretto Liqueur
1/4 ounce of Sloe Gin liqueur
1/4 ounce of Triple Sec Liqueur
1/4 ounce of Vodka
1 ounce of Gatorade Island Burst
2 Shot Glass
Finely crushed Salted Carmel Candy for (**Rim
Of Shot Glass)**
Chase with 1 ounce shot glass of Gatorade
Sport Mix (Island Burst)

•Wet the rim of your shot glass.. when ready...
dip your rim of shot glass into Finely crushed
Salted Carmel candy...

•Slowly...add your Liqueur and Vodka..to your shot
glass...in your other shot glass...**Chase with 1
ounce shot of Gatorade Island Burst Sport drink**
Cheers...Enjoy!

Impaired   Tipsy   Love it!   DD

Don't
Drink and Drive
Stop

Feel Me up!

1/2 ounce of Jagermeister Liqueur
1/2 ounce of Black Sambuca Liqueur
 Shot Glass
Splash of Lemon Gin
  Cheers...Enjoy!

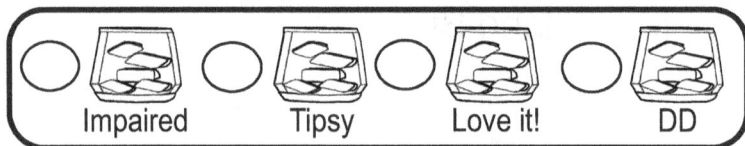

○ Impaired	○ Tipsy	○ Love it!	○ DD

Freak... Gummy Bear

1/3 ounce of Cherry Vodka
1/3 ounce of Peach Schnapps Liqueur
1/3 ounce of Sour Puss Raspberry
Shot Glass
Sour Gummy Bear to garnish
Splash of Grenadine
  Cheers...Enjoy!

○ Impaired	○ Tipsy	○ Love it!	○ DD

58

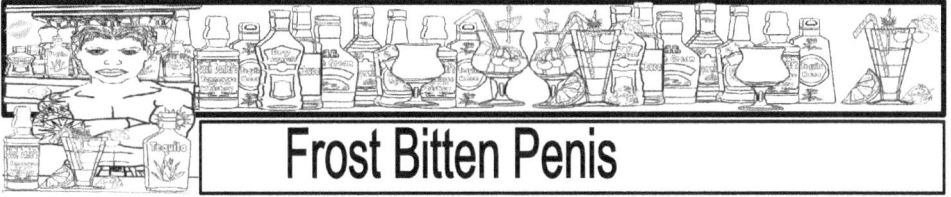

Frost Bitten Penis

- 1 ounce of Silver Tequila
- 1/2 ounce of Blue Curacao Liqueur
- 1/2 ounce of Chocolate Liqueur
- 1/2 ounce of Creme de Menthe Liqueur
- Fancy Large Cocktail Glass
- Add Ice Cubes
- Fill Cocktail Glass with Heavy Cream or
- Vanilla Flavoured Milk
- Splash of Diet Root Beer
- 6-10 inch Paper Straw

- Grabbing hold of Cocktail shaker ..add all your liqueur...and Tequila... Do not eject yet...wait...slowly in a rhythmic motion... shake...shake...
- Add wet cold slippery ice cubes...shake...
- Holding tightly... grabbing the top edge... pour slowly... releasing into your Fancy Glass...Add a splash of Diet Root Beer....
- Quickly insert your large 6-10 inch thick Paper Straw...hold...release... Cheers...Enjoy!

| Impaired | Tipsy | Love it! | DD |

Don't
Drink and Drive!
Stop

Friday...TGIF!

1/3 ounce of Tequila Rose Liqueur
1/3 ounce of Bailey's Irish Cream Liqueur
1/3 ounce of Grand Marnier Liqueur
 Shot Glass
1 Bud Light Beer Chaser!
   Cheers...Enjoy!

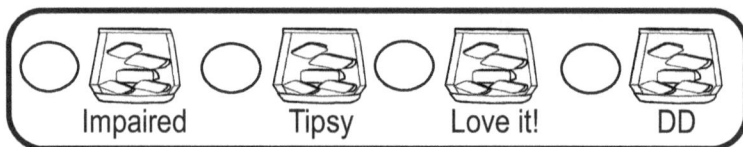

Impaired		Tipsy		Love it!		DD

Fuck Me Silly!

1/2 ounce of Captain Morgans Rum
1/2 ounce of Silver Tequila
2 Tbsp of Sugar
Pinch of Pink Salt
 Shot Glass *(Sugar and Salted Your Rim)*
Lemon Wedge **to Suck on**
   1 Red Head (or Hair Colour of your Choice)
   Cheers...Enjoy!

Impaired		Tipsy		Love it!		DD

60

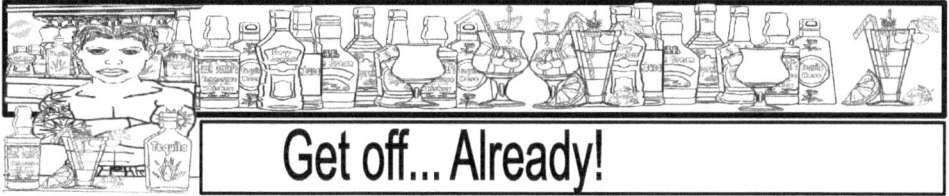

Get off... Already!

- 1/4 ounce of Godiva Chocolate Liqueur
- 1/4 ounce of Goldschlager Liqueur
- 1/4 ounce of Grand Marnier Liqueur
- 1/4 ounce of Irish Cream Liqueur
- Fancy Ass Cocktail Glass
- Add Ice Cubes
- Fill Glass with Heavy Cream or Vanilla Flavoured Milk
- Splash of Coke or Sprite
- 6-10 inch Paper Straw

- Grabbing hold of Cocktail Shaker...add all your Liquor....and top Shaker with Heavy Cream or Vanilla flavoured Milk...
- Add your ice cubes...Do not eject yet... wait...slowly in a rhythmic motion...shake shake...Hold tightly...grab the top edge... pour slowly...releasing into your Cocktail Glass...Add a splash of Coke or Sprite...
- Quickly insert your large 6-10 inch thick Paper straw...hold...release Cheers... Enjoy!

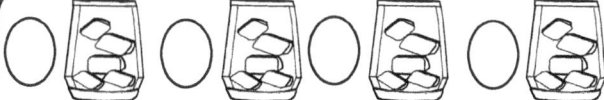

| Impaired | Tipsy | Love it! | DD |

Don't Drink and Drive
Stop

61

Good Bye... Lover!

1/2 ounce of Cinnamon Tequila
1/2 ounce of Vanilla Vodka (Absolut)
Shot Glass *(Wet Rim)*
Grenadine *(for Rim)*
Cinnamon Candy Hearts (Finely Crushed)
Dip Shot Glass Rim into <u>Grenadine</u> then into Crushed Cinnamon Hearts...Fill Shot Glass with Tequila and Vanilla Vodka...**1-2-3 Goodbye** Cheers...Enjoy!

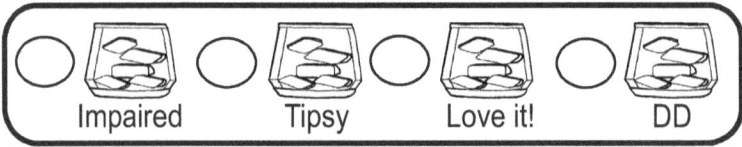

| ○ | Impaired | ○ | Tipsy | ○ | Love it! | ○ | DD |

Giggles

1/3 ounce of Blue Curacao
1/3 ounce of Yukon Jack Whiskey
1/3 ounce of Galliano Liqueur
Shot Glass

What is the difference between Bud Light and Sex in a Canoe? "Nothing, they're both Fucking Close to water"!

| Impaired | Tipsy | Love it! | DD |

Goody Two Shoes

1/3 ounce of Crown Royal Whiskey
1/3 ounce of Sour Apple Schnapps
1/3 ounce of Cranberry Juice
Shot Glass
Splash of Diet Coke
Cheers...Enjoy!

Impaired	Tipsy	Love it!	DD

Green Leprechaun..WTF!

1/3 ounce of Irish Whiskey
1/3 ounce of Melon Liqueur
1/3 ounce of White Mint Liqueur (Marie Brizard)
Shot Glass
Whipped Cream *(Cool Whip)*
Top Shot Glass with Cool Whip
Drizzle a little bit of Melon Liqueur on top of
Cool Whip...
One Leprechaun Hat

Impaired	Tipsy	Love it!	DD

Don't
Drink and Drive!
Stop

63

Gilligan's Island... Hard On

1 ounce of Citrus Vodka (Burnett's)
1 ounce of Coconut Tequila (1800 Coconut)
1/2 ounce of Mango Liqueur (Somras)
Sexy Cocktail Glass
Top with Pineapple Juice
Splash of Cranberry Juice
Cherries and Pineapple Wedge for garnish
Spear Stir Stick for garnish
6-10 inch Paper Straw
1 Mary Ann

- Grabbing hold of Cocktail Shaker...add your Vodka... Tequila...Mango Liqueur...
- Top with Pineapple Juice...and splash of Cranberry Juice... Do not eject yet... wait...slowly in a rhythmic motion..shake...
- Fill with wet cold slippery cubes ...Holding tightly... grab the top edge of shaker... pour slowly...releasing into your Sexy Cocktail Glass...Garnish with a Pineapple Wedge and Cherries ...Quickly insert your large
- 6-10 inch thick Paper straw... Cheers... Enjoy!

Impaired   Tipsy   Love it!   DD

64

Grapefruit Margarita

1 1/2 ounces of Silver Tequila
1/2 ounce of Triple Sec Liqueur
Margarita Glass
Add Ice Cubes
1/2 Teaspoon of Lime Juice
Splash of Red Grapefruit Juice
Top with Ginger Ale
Pinch of Pink Salt
2 Tbsp of Sugar (for Rim)
2 Tbsp of Zest from a Grapefruit (for Rim)
2 Tbsp of Zest from a Lime (for Rim)
Grapefruit Wedge on a Spear Stir Stick
6-10 inch Paper Straw

- *Sprinkle 2 tbsp Sugar and pinch of Salt... wide on a plate .... In an even layer.. add your Grapefruit Zest and Lime Zest to taste.....*
- With your Fingers take the Lime Wedge and slowly go around the Margarita rim......until a perfectly moisten rim...Gently grab the rim of the Margarita Glass and tilt into Sugar and Salt Margarita mixture
- With a Cocktail shaker add your liquids and ice...
- Shake...strain...into *(Sugar Rimmed)* Margarita Glass
- Garnish with Grapefruit Wedge...
- 6-10 inch Straw... Enjoy!

Impaired   Tipsy   Love it!   DD

Don't
Drink and Drive!
Stop

65

Golden Shower

- 1 ounce of Vodka
- 1/2 ounce of Triple Sec Liqueur
- Fancy Ass Cocktail Glass
- Wet Chilled Ice Cubes
- Top Orange Juice
- Orange Wedge and Cherries for Garnish
- Splash of Ginger Ale
- 6-10 inch Paper Straw

- Grabbing hold of Cocktail Shaker add your Triple Sec and Vodka...Top with Orange Juice
- Do not eject yet...wait...slowly in a rhythmic motion shake...shake...
- Fill with wet cold slippery cubes. Holding tightly...grabbing the top edge of shaker...pour slowly...releasing into your Fancy Ass Glass
- Add a splash of Ginger Ale...
- Garnish with a Orange Wedge and Cherries Quickly insert your 6-10 inch Paper Straw...Cheers...Enjoy!

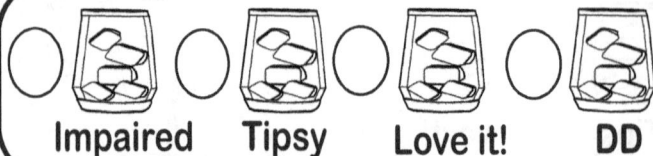

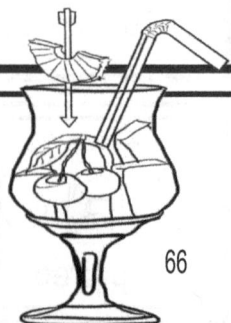

Impaired   Tipsy   Love it!   DD

66

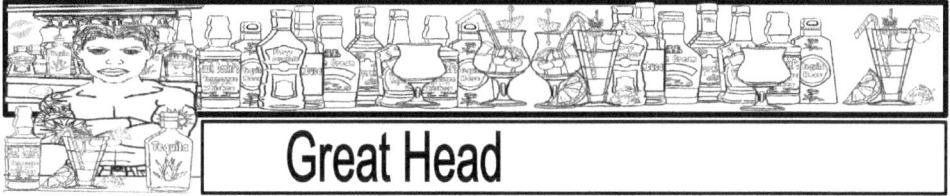

Great Head

- 1 ounce of Crown Royal Whiskey
- 1/2 ounce of Peppermint Schnapps
- 1/2 ounce of Bailey's Irish Cream
- Fancy Ass Cocktail Glass
- Wet Chilled Ice Cubes
- Top with Heavy Cream
- 6-9 Cherries for Garnish
- Spear Stir Stick for Cherries
- 6-10 inch Paper Straw

- Grabbing hold of the Cocktail Shaker ..add Crown Royal... Schnapps... Bailey's... Fill with wet cold slippery cubes..Top with Cream
- Shake...do not eject yet...wait...slowly in a rhythmic motion... grabbing the top edge of shaker strain... pour slowly...releasing into your Fancy Ass Glass...
- Garnish with Cherries..Quickly insert your large 6-10 inch thick Paper straw... Cheers... Enjoy!

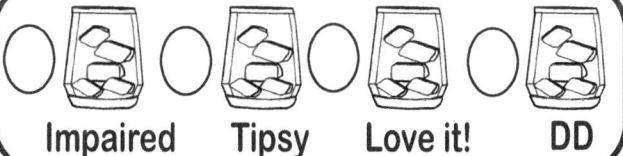

Impaired   Tipsy   Love it!   DD

Don't Drink and Drive! Stop

67

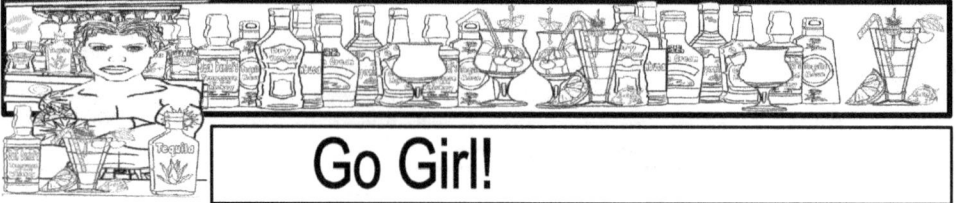

Go Girl!

🍓1/2 ounce of Jagermeister Liqueur
🍓1/2 ounce of Butterscotch Liqueur
🍓Shot Glass
   Cheers...Enjoy!

Impaired   Tipsy   Love it!   DD

Happy Hooker

🍓1/2 ounce of Creme de Banana Liqueur
🍓1/2 ounce of Creme de Cafe Liqueur
🍓Whipped Cream (**top rim with Whipped Cream**)
🍓Shot Glass
   Cheers...Enjoy!

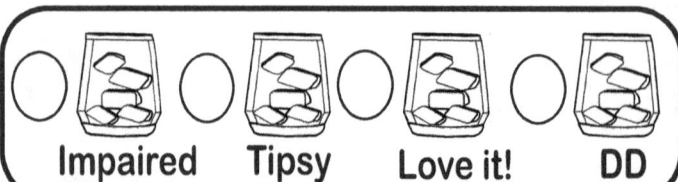

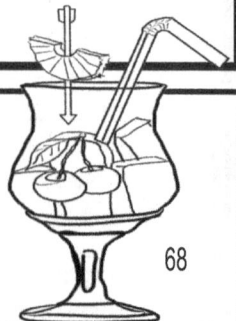

Impaired   Tipsy   Love it!   DD

Hey... Mr Sunshine

- 1/3 ounce of Jameson Irish Whiskey
- 1/3 ounce of Peach Schnapps Liqueur
- 1/3 ounce of Lemon Vodka (Absolut)
- Splash of Lemon Lime Soda
- *Sugar Rimmed Shot Glass*
- Cheers...Enjoy!

	Impaired		Tipsy		Love it!		DD
○		○		○		○	

Hawaii Tourist Buzz

- 1/2 ounce of White Rum
- 1/2 ounce of Mango Liqueur (J.F. Haden's)
- Splash of Pineapple Juice
- Splash of Grenadine Syrup
- Shot Glass
- Cheers...Enjoy!

Impaired		Tipsy		Love it!		DD
	○		○		○	

Don't
Drink and Drive
Stop

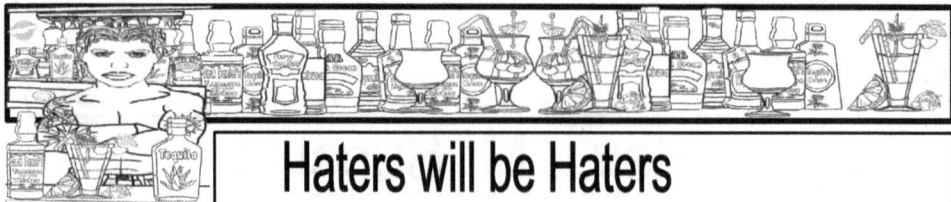

Haters will be Haters

🍓 1/3 ounce of Creme de Cacao Liqueur
🍓 1/3 ounce of Creme de Menthe Liqueur
🍓 1/3 ounce of Chocolate Vodka (360 Double)
🍓 Shot Glass
Cheers...Enjoy!

Hey Babe...what's your sign?
Do not Enter!

Impaired   Tipsy   Love it!   DD

Hell Valentine's Day...Fuck!

🍓 1/3 ounce of Cherry Vodka (Smirnoff)
🍓 1/3 ounce of Mozart Chocolate Liqueur
🍓 1/3 ounce of Silver Tequila
🍓 Finely Crushed Cinnamon Hearts to
Rim your Shot Glass *(wet your Rim in Grenadine then dip into Hearts)*
Cheers...Enjoy!

Impaired   Tipsy   Love it!   DD

70

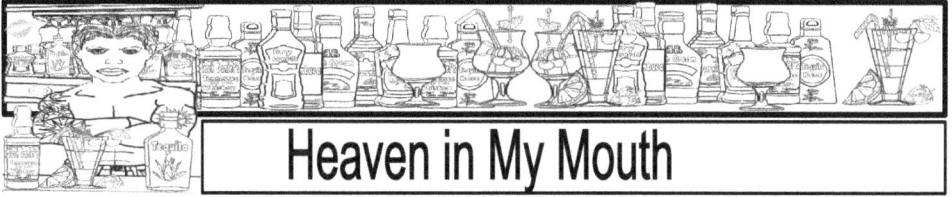

Heaven in My Mouth

1 ounce of Malibu Rum
1/2 ounce of Raspberry Rum (Parrot Bay)
Fancy Ass Cocktail Glass
Wet Chilled Ice Cubes
Top Glass with Hawaiian Punch
Splash of Ginger Ale or Tonic Water
Garnish with Pineapple Wedge and Cherries
Spear Stir Stick for garnish
6-10 inch Paper Straw

- Grabbing hold of a Cocktail Shaker add your Rum.. Top with Hawaiian Punch...and splash of Ginger Ale and add ice cubes to Shaker...
- Cover and shake well..pour into your Fancy Ass Cocktail Glass.....
- Insert your 6-10 inch Paper Straw
- Garnish with Pineapple Wedge and Cherries Cheers...Enjoy!

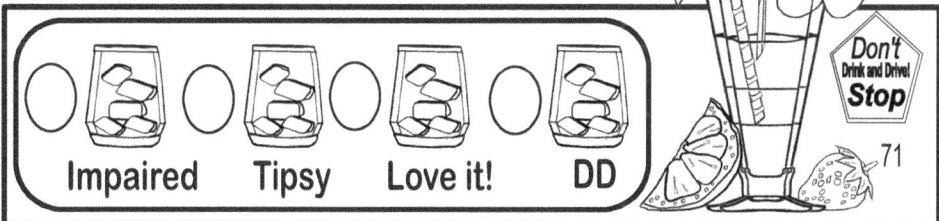

Impaired   Tipsy   Love it!   DD

Don't
Drink and Drive!
Stop

71

Hello Nurse

- 1 ounce of Vodka
- 1/2 ounce of Amaretto Liqueur
- Sexy Ass Cocktail Glass
- Top with Chocolate or Strawberry Milk
- Whipped Cream *(Cool Whip)*
- Drizzle some Chocolate or Strawberry Syrup *(On top of Cool Whip)*
- 6-9 Cherries on Spear Stir Stick
- 6-10 inch Red and White Striped Paper Straw

- Grabbing hold of a Cocktail Shaker ..add all your Liquor...Top with Strawberry Milk... Do not eject yet...wait...slowly in a rhythmic motion shake... Fill with wet cold slippery cubes ...Holding tightly grabbing the top edge of shaker...pour slowly...releasing liquids into your Fancy Cocktail Glass
- Top Sexy Glass with Cool Whip...Drizzle Strawberry Syrup on top of Cool Whip....
- Quickly insert your large 6-10 inch thick Paper straw...hold...release... Cheers... Enjoy!

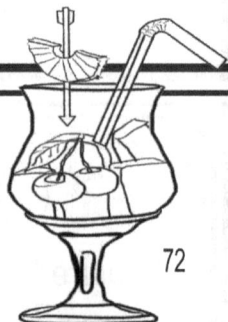

Impaired   Tipsy   Love it!   DD

72

Holiday Hangover

- 2 ounces of Bacardi White Rum
- 1/2 ounce of Kahlua Liqueur
- Fancy Ass Cocktail Glass
- Crushed Ice Cubes
- Top with Egg Nog
- Splash of Milk
- 6-10 inch Red and Green Paper Straw
- *1 Candy Cane*

- Grabbing hold of a Cocktail Shaker add your Liquor... top with Egg Nog and a Splash of Milk
- Add ice cubes to a Cocktail Shaker... Cover and shake well..strain...pour into your Fancy Ass Cocktail Glass.....
- Insert your 6-10 inch Paper Straw...
- Garnish with a Candy Cane and Serve... Cheers...Enjoy!
  Merry Ho Ho!

Impaired   Tipsy   Love it!   DD

Don't Drink and Drive! Stop

73

Horney Melon Baller

1 ounce of Melon Liqueur
1/2 ounce of White Rum
1/2 ounce of Vodka
Fancy Ass Cocktail Glass
Wet Cold Ice Cubes
Top with Sprite
Add Splash of Grenadine Syrup
Add Splash of Ginger Ale
6-10 inch Paper Straw

- Grabbing hold of Cocktail Shaker ..add Melon Liqueur... Rum... Vodka...Top with Sprite
- Do not eject yet...wait...slowly in a rhythmic motion...shake... Fill with wet cold slippery cubes...Hold tightly grabbing the top edge...
- Pour slowly...releasing into your Fancy Ass Glass...Add a splash of Grenadine...splash of Ginger Ale...
- Quickly insert your 6-10 inch straw... hold...release...Cheers... Enjoy!

Impaired   Tipsy   Love it!   DD

74

Hot and Spicy Men...FML

1 ounce of Captain Morgan Spiced Rum
1/2 ounce of Jack Daniel's Whiskey
1/2 ounce of Jim Beam Whiskey
1/2 ounce of Peppermint Schnapps
Fancy Ass Cocktail Glass
Wet Chilled Ice Cubes
Top Cocktail Glass with Dr. Pepper
Splash of Ginger Ale or Tonic Water
6-10 inch Straw

- Grabbing hold of Cocktail Shaker ..add all your Liquor... Top with Dr. Pepper... Do not eject yet...wait...slowly in a rhythmic motion...shake..
- Fill with wet cold slippery cubes *(optional)* ...
- Hold tightly... grabbing the top edge of Shaker... pour slowly...releasing into your Fancy Cocktail Glass...Splash of Ginger Ale...
- Quickly insert your 6-10 inch straw... hold...release...Cheers...Enjoy!

Impaired   Tipsy   Love it!   DD

Don't
Drink and Drive!
Stop

Horney Toad

1 ounce of Triple Sec Liqueur
1/2 ounce of Kahlua Liqueur
1/2 ounce of Chocolate Tequila (Olmeca)
Fancy Ass Cocktail Glass
Add Ice Cubes
Top Cocktail Glass with Chocolate Milk
Add Splash of Heavy Cream
***Spray some Whipped Cream on top of Glass
Drizzle some Bols Peppermint Liqueur
On top of the Whipped Cream (Cool Whip)***
6-10 inch Paper Straw

- Fill your Cocktail Shaker with cold wet ice cubes...Add Triple Sec...Kahlua...Tequila...
- Splash of Heavy Cream...Gently shake... release your liquids into your Sexy Ass Cocktail Glass...Top your Fancy Glass with Whipped Cream and add drizzle of Peppermint Liqueur on top...
- Garnish with Cherries...
- insert your 6-10 inch Paper Straw Cheers...Enjoy!

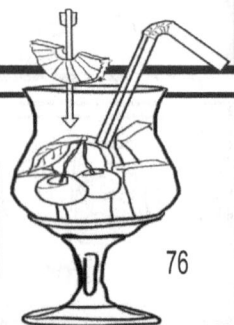

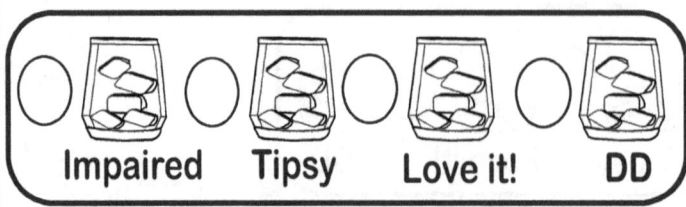

Impaired   Tipsy   Love it!   DD

Kamikaze

1/2 ounce of Vodka
1/2 ounce of Orange Liqueur (Contreau)
Fancy Cocktail Glass
Add Ice Cubes
Top Cocktail Glass with Orange Juice
Add Splash of Fresh Lime Juice
Cherries for Garnish on a Spear Stir Stick
6-10 inch Paper Straw
Cheers...Enjoy!

Impaired	Tipsy	Love it!	DD

Killer Buns

1/3 ounce of Bailey's Irish Cream
1/3 ounce of Creme de Menthe Liqueur
1/3 ounce of Black Sambuca
Shot Glass
Cheers...Enjoy!

Impaired	Tipsy	Love it!	DD

Don't Drink and Drive! **Stop**

Lovers

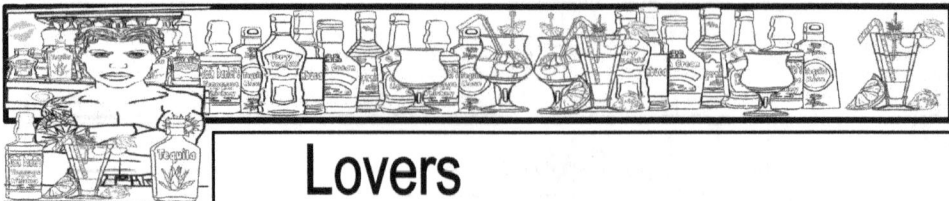

1/2 ounce of Tequila Rose Liqueur
1/2 ounce of Jagermeister Liqueur
Shot Glass
Cheers...Enjoy!

| Impaired | | Tipsy | | Love it! | | DD | |

Long Laster

1/2 ounce of Silver Tequila
1/2 ounce of Southern Comfort
Shot Glass
Fancy Cocktail Glass
1 Can of Red Bull
Fill Fancy Cocktail Glass with Red Bull
Drop gently your Liquor filled Shot Glass into the Red Bull filled Fancy Cocktail Glass
Cheers...Enjoy!

| Impaired | Tipsy | Love it! | DD |

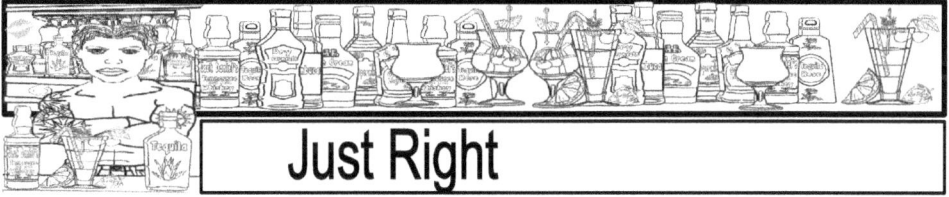

1/2 ounce of Kahlua Liqueur
1/2 ounce of Irish Cream Liqueur
Shot Glass
   Cheers...Enjoy!

Impaired   Tipsy   Love it!   DD

Jerk Off

1/4 ounce of Bailey's Irish Cream
1/4 ounce of Jagermeister Liqueur
1/4 ounce of Peppermint Schnapps
1/4 ounce of Grand Marnier Liqueur
Shot Glass
   Cheers...Enjoy!

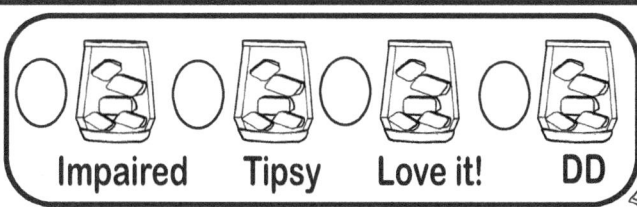

Impaired   Tipsy   Love it!   DD

Don't
Drink and Drive!
Stop

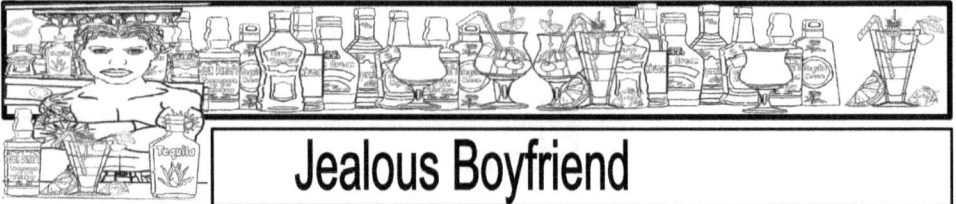

Jealous Boyfriend

1/3 ounce of Silver Tequila
1/3 ounce of Southern Comfort
1/3 ounce of Amaretto Liqueur
Shot Glass
Cheers...Enjoy!

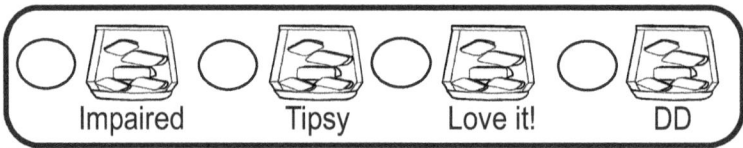

Impaired	Tipsy	Love it!	DD

Just Be Over

1/3 ounce of Melon Liqueur
1/3 ounce of Goldschlager Liqueur
1/3 Pineapple Juice
Splash of Grenadine Syrup
Shot Glass (Dipped in Grenadine and Sugar)
Cheers...Enjoy!

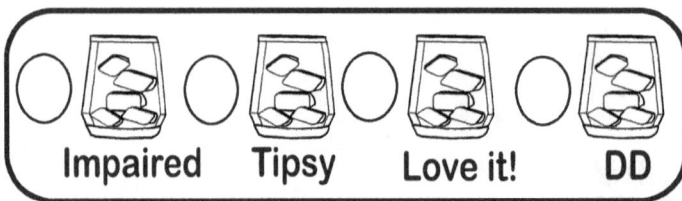

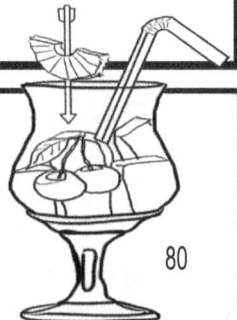

Impaired	Tipsy	Love it!	DD

Melania Martini

1/2 ounce of Creme De Cacao Dark Liqueur
1/2 ounce of Vanilla Vodka
1/2 ounce of Bailey's Irish Cream Liqueur
1/2 ounce of Kahlua Liqueur
Martini Glass
Top Martini Glass with Vanilla Flavoured
   Milk or Heavy Cream
Splash of Diet Coke
Top Martini Glass with Whipped Cream
Shot Glass with 1 ounce of Silver Tequila
Chase with Tequila shot

- Fill your Cocktail Shaker with cold wet ice cubes
- Add your Vodka...and your liqueur... Top with
  Milk or Heavy Cream...Gently shake in a up and
  down motion... release and strain... Pour into your
  Sexy Martini Glass...Splash of Diet Coke and
  top Martini Glass with Whipped Cream...
- Garnish with Cherries...
- Insert your 6-10 inch red Paper straw...
- **Chase with a shot of Tequila**
  Cheers...Enjoy!

Impaired   Tipsy   Love it!   DD

Don't Drink and Drive! **Stop**

81

Malibu Barbie

1 ounce of Malibu Coconut Rum
1/2 ounce of Pineapple Rum
1/2 ounce of Raspberry Vodka
Martini Glass
Top Martini Glass with Cream Soda Pop
Splash of Grenadine Syrup
Strawberries and Cherries for Garnish
Spear Stir Stick for Garnish
Spray Glass with Pink **_Food Grade_** Sparkles
Pink Cocktail Umbrella
Cheers...Enjoy!

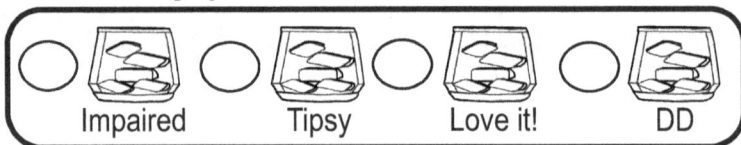

Impaired   Tipsy   Love it!   DD

Meat Head

1/2 ounce of Scotch
1/2 ounce of Silver Tequila
Shot Glass
Cheers...Enjoy!

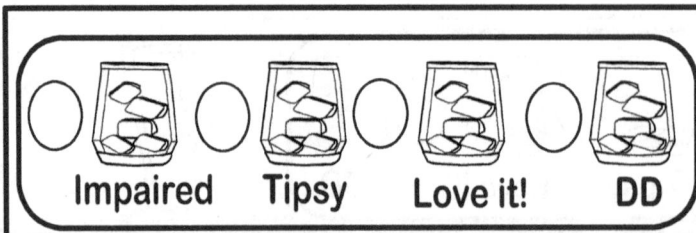

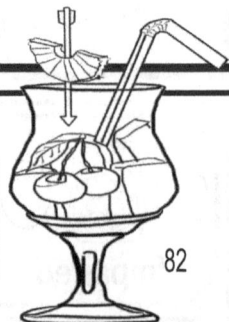

Impaired   Tipsy   Love it!   DD

82

Mountain Dew Me

1 ounce of Melon Liqueur
1/2 ounce of Triple Sec Liqueur
Fancy Cocktail Glass
Add Ice Cubes
Top Cocktail Glass with Mountain Dew
Splash of Pineapple Juice
Lime Wedge and Melon Slice for Garnish
Spear Stir Stick for the Garnish
6-10 inch Paper Straw
Cheers...Enjoy!

Impaired	Tipsy	Love it!	DD
○	○	○	○

Move Over

1/2 ounce of Raspberry Sour Puss Liqueur
1/2 ounce of Southern Comfort
Shot Glass
Cheers...Enjoy!

Impaired	Tipsy	Love it!	DD

Don't Drink and Drive!
Stop

Pink Tequila Buzz

1 ounce of Silver Tequila
1/2 ounce of Strawberry Bailey's Liqueur
Fancy Ass Cocktail Glass
Add Ice Cubes
Top with Tonic Water or Ginger Ale
1/2 Cup of Strawberries (blended)
1/2 Cup of Watermelon (blended)
2 Limes Wedges (juiced)
1 Tbsp of Agave Nectar (optional)
Strawberries and Watermelon Wedge
6-10 inch Paper Straw

- In a Blender...combine Strawberries and Watermelon
- Add Juice from Lime Wedges and all other Spirits.
- Add the Agave (Optional)... blend to a smoothie consistency...
- Place all ingredients into Cocktail Shaker ...
- Shake then strain into the Sexy Ass Cocktail Glass..(add ice cubes if you wish)
- Top with Tonic Water or Ginger Ale...add Strawberries and Watermelon Wedge for Garnish
- Insert your your 6-10 inch Paper straw... Cheers... Enjoy!

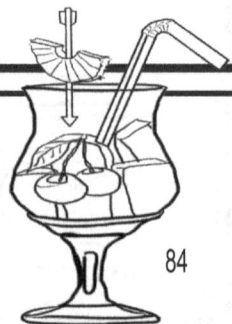

Impaired   Tipsy   Love it!   DD

84

Porn Star

- 1 ounce of Raspberry Sour Puss Liqueur
- 1/2 ounce of Blue Curacao Liqueur
- Top with Sprite or Tonic Water
- Fancy Ass Cocktail Glass
- Add Ice Cubes
- Spear Stir Stick
- 6-9 Cherries for Garnish
- 6-10 inch Black Paper Straw

- Fill your Cocktail Shaker with cold wet ice cubes...
- Add your Sour Puss and Curacao and top with Sprite...
- Gently shake...in an up and down motion...release and eject liquids from Cocktail Shaker... into your Sexy Ass Glass...
- Garnish with Cherries...
- Insert your 6-10 inch Black Straw...
- Cheers...Enjoy

Impaired   Tipsy   Love it!   DD

Don't Drink and Drive
Stop

85

Paralyzer

1 ounce of Vodka
1/2 ounce of Kahlua Coffee Liqueur
Fancy Cocktail Glass
Add Ice Cubes
Top with Cola or Diet Cola
Splash of Heavy Cream or Milk
Whipped Cream *(top of Cocktail Glass)*
Cherries on Spear Stir Stick for Garnish
6-10 inch Paper Straw

- Fill your Cocktail Shaker with cold and wet ice cubes...
- Add your Vodka and Kahlua liqueur and top with Diet Cola...
- Gently shake...in an up and down motion...release...and eject liquids from Cocktail Shaker...and pour into your Sexy Cocktail Glass...Add a splash of Heavy Cream... Top with a spray of Whipped Cream to the top of Fancy Cocktail Glass...
- Garnish with Cherries ...
- Insert your 6-10 inch Paper Straw... Cheers...Enjoy!

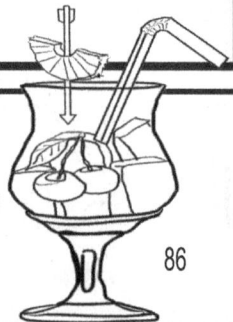

Impaired   Tipsy   Love it!   DD

86

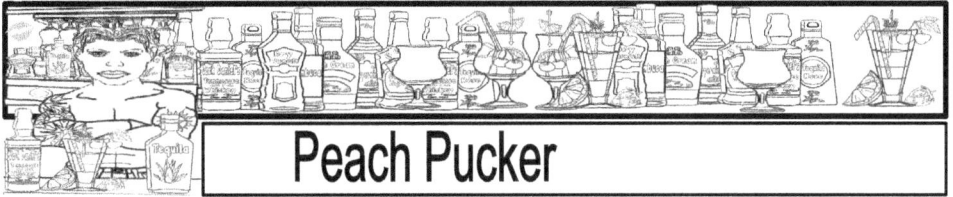

Peach Pucker

1/2 ounce of Vodka
1/2 ounce Peach Schnapps Liqueur
Fancy Ass Cocktail Glass
Add Crushed Ice Cubes
1/2 Glass of Cranberry Juice
1/2 Glass of 7-Up or Tonic Water
Splash of Grapefruit Juice
Peach Wedge and Cherries for Garnish
Spear Stir Stick
6-10 inch Paper Straw

- Fill your Cocktail Shaker with cold and wet ice cubes...
- Add your Vodka and Peach Schnapps...Top with 7-UP and your Cranberry juice...
- With your Shaker...Gently shake...In an up and down motion... release...and eject liquids from Cocktail Shaker...and pour into your Fancy Cocktail Glass...Add a Splash of Grapefruit Juice...
- Garnish with Peach wedge and Cherries ...
- Insert your 6-10 inch Paper Straw... Cheers...Enjoy!

Impaired   Tipsy   Love it!   DD

Don't
Drink and Drive
Stop

87

Saturday Slammer

1 ounce of Pineapple Rum
1/4 ounce of Strawberry Rum
1/4 ounce of Coconut Rum
1/4 ounce of Blue Curacao Liqueur
Sexy Cocktail Glass
Add Ice Cubes
Top with Orange Juice
Splash of Pineapple Juice
Splash of Grenadine Syrup
6-9 Cherries for Garnish
Spear Stir Stick for Cherries
6-10 inch Paper Straw

- Fill your Cocktail Shaker with cold and wet ice cubes...
- Add your Rum and Blue Curacao...Top with Orange Juice and splash of Pineapple Juice to the Cocktail Shaker...
- With your Shaker gently shake...In an up and down motion... release...and eject liquids ..and pour into your Sexy Ass Cocktail Glass...
- Add a Splash of Grenadine...
- Garnish with Cherries ...insert your 6-10 inch Paper Straw... Cheers...Enjoy!

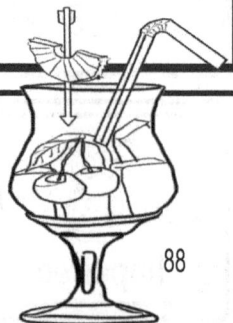

Impaired   Tipsy   Love it!   DD

88

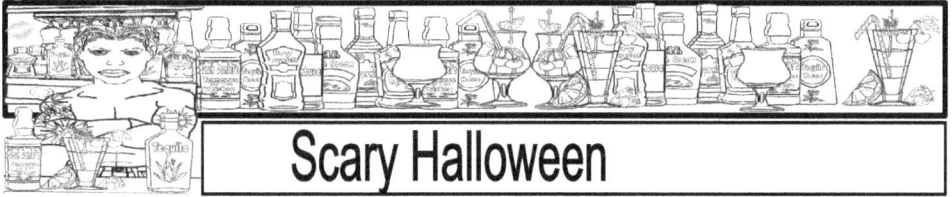

Scary Halloween

1 ounce Black Sambuca Liqueur
1 ounce of ounce Whipped Vodka(Pinnacle)
Scary Sexy Cocktail Glass
Add Ice Cubes
Top with Ginger Ale or Tonic Water
Splash of Simple Syrup*(Recipe page-2)*
6-9 Black Cherries for Garnish
Scary Cocktail Umbrella for Garnish
Spear Stir Stick for Cherries
6-10 inch Paper Straw

- Fill your Cocktail Shaker with cold and wet ice cubes...
- Add your Sambuca and Whipped Vodka ... Top with Ginger
  Ale... Splash of Simple Syrup into the Cocktail Shaker.....Gently
  shake...in an up and down motion...release...and eject liquids
  from Cocktail Shaker...and pour into your Sexy Cocktail Glass...
- Garnish with Black Cherries and Scary Cocktail Umbrella ...
- Insert your 6-10 inch Black Paper Straw...
  Cheers...Enjoy!

Impaired   Tipsy   Love it!   DD

Don't
Drink and Drive!
Stop

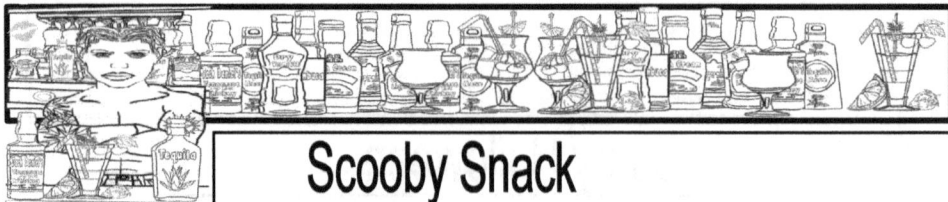

Scooby Snack

1 ounce of Melon Liqueur
1/4 ounce of Malibu Rum
1/4 ounce of Bailey's Irish Cream Liqueur
1/4 ounce of Banana Schnapps Liqueur
1/4 ounce of Parrot Bay Pineapple Rum
Fancy Cocktail Glass
Add Ice Cubes
Top Glass with Diet Sprite or Sprite
6-9 Cherries For Garnish
Spear Stir Stick for Garnish
6-10 inch Paper Straw

- Fill your Cocktail Shaker with the Liquor ...
- Top Cocktail Glass with Diet Sprite or Sprite...
- Add wet cold ice cubes... in rhythmic motion.. shake..Grip the rim tight...holding.. and slowly release liquid from Cocktail Shaker...Wait......wait slowly.... eject into Fancy Ass Cocktail Glass
- Garnish with Cherries on a Spear Stir Stick
- Quickly insert your 6-10 inch (paper) thick Straw... Suck back gently and Enjoy!
1 Super Shaggy Sandwich

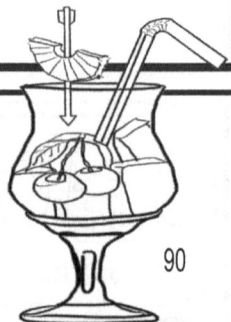

Impaired   Tipsy   Love it!   DD

Spicy Strawberry Kiss

🍓 1 ounce of Jalapeño Tequila
🍓 1/2 ounce of Vodka
🍓 Margarita Cocktail Glass
🍓 Add Ice Cubes
🍓 Splash of Strawberry Syrup
🍓 Top with Simple Syrup *(Recipe page-2)*
🍓 Splash of freshly Squeezed Lime Juice
🍓 Margarita Salted Rim *(Recipe page-3)*
🍓 6-9 Jalapeños Peppers for Garnish
🍓 6-10 Paper Straw

●Fill your Cocktail Shaker with Tequila and Vodka
●Top the Cocktail Glass (*Salted Rim*)... Splash of
  Simple Syrup... splash of Lime Juice...Add wet
  cold ice cubes... In rhythmic motion...shake...grip
  the rim tight...holding... release liquid from Cocktail
  Shaker...wait....wait... slowly.... eject into Fancy
  Ass Cocktail Glass...Splash of Strawberry Syrup...
●Garnish with Jalapeño's on a Spear Stir Stick
●Quickly insert your 6-10 inch (paper) thick Straw...
  Suck back gently and Enjoy!

Impaired   Tipsy   Love it!   DD

Don't
Drink and Drive
Stop

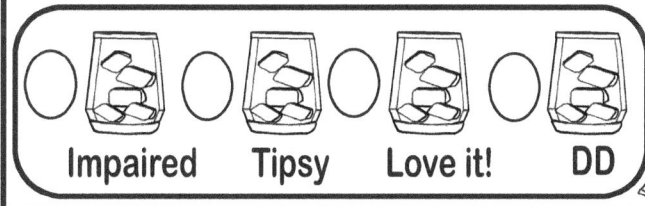

91

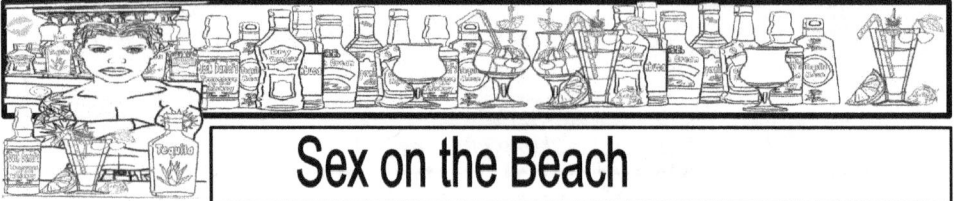

Sex on the Beach

1 ounce of Vodka
1/2 ounce of Peach Schnapps Liqueur
Sexy Cocktail Glass
Add Ice Cubes
1/2 Glass of Orange Juice
1/2 Glass of Cranberry Juice
Splash of Sprite
Pineapple Wedge and Cherries on a
Spear Stir Stick
6-10 inch Paper Straw
Cheers...Enjoy!

Impaired   Tipsy   Love it!   DD

Silly Ginny

1/2 ounce of Gin
1/2 ounce of Sloe Gin
Splash of Grenadine Syrup
Shot Glass
Cheers...Enjoy!

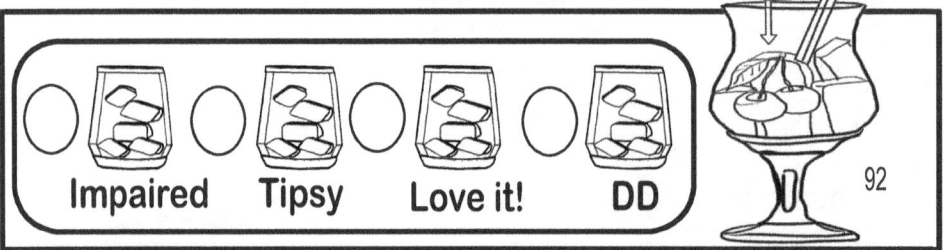

Impaired   Tipsy   Love it!   DD

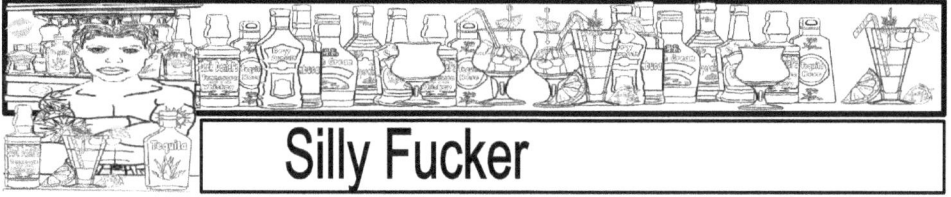

Silly Fucker

- 1 ounce of Tequila Gold
- Shot Glass
- Red Bull Energy Drink
- **_1 Silly Fucker_**
  Cheers...Enjoy!

Do not try this at home!

Impaired   Tipsy   Love it!   DD

Sweet Load

- 1/2 ounce of Bailey's Strawberry Cream Liqueur
- 1/2 ounce of Bailey's Salted Carmel
- Whipped Cream (Cool Whip)
- **Top Shot Glass with Whipped Cream**
- Shot Glass
  Cheers...Enjoy!

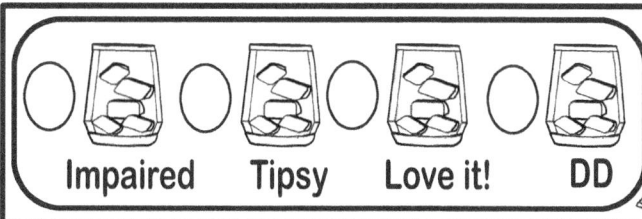

Impaired   Tipsy   Love it!   DD

Don't Drink and Drive! **Stop**

Slow Safe Sex

- 1/3 ounce of Bailey's Irish Cream Liqueur
- 1/3 ounce of Malibu Rum
- 1/3 ounce of Whiskey
- 2 Shot Glasses
- ***Chase with 1 ounce Shot of Citron Vodka (Absolut)***
  Cheers...Enjoy!

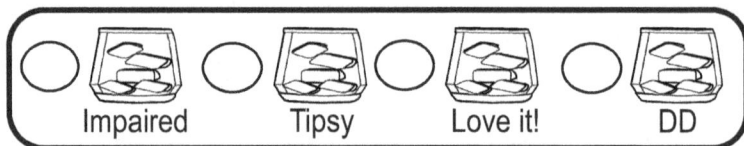

| ○ | Impaired | ○ | Tipsy | ○ | Love it! | ○ | DD |

Shut the Fuck Up!

- 1/2 ounce of Captain Morgans Spiced Rum
- 1/2 ounce of Butter Ripple Liqueur
- Shot Glass
  Cheers...Enjoy!

| ○ | Impaired | ○ | Tipsy | ○ | Love it! | ○ | DD |

94

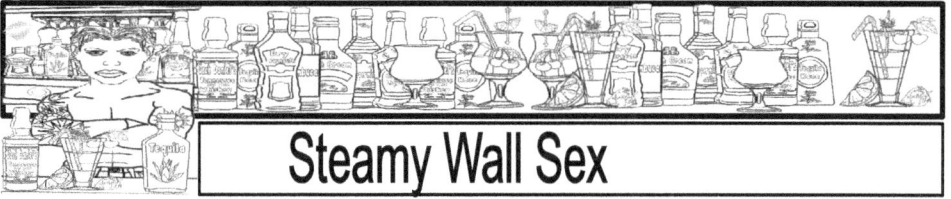

Steamy Wall Sex

1/3 ounce of Kahlua Liqueur
1/3 ounce of Bailey's Irish Cream
Liqueur
1/3 ounce of Vodka
Shot Glass
Cheers...Enjoy!

Impaired   Tipsy   Love it!   DD

Sniff Me

1/3 ounce of Jose Cuervo Tequila
1/3 ounce of Jack Daniel's Whiskey
1/3 ounce of Vodka
Shot Glass
Cheers...Enjoy!

Impaired   Tipsy   Love it!   DD

Don't
Drink and Drive!
Stop

95

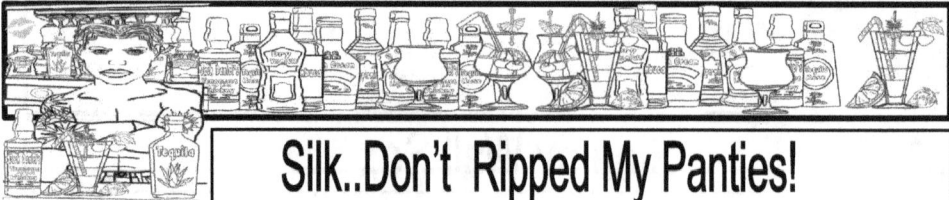

Silk..Don't Ripped My Panties!

- 1 ounce of Silver Tequila
- 1/2 ounce of Cointreau Liqueur
- 1/2 ounce of Marie Brizard Liqueur (Banana)
- Sexy Cocktail Glass
- Add Ice Cubes
- Top Cocktail Glass with Tonic Water or Sprite
- Splash of Lime Juice
- Cherries for Garnish
- Spear Stir Stick for Cherries
- 6-10 inch Paper Straw
- Cheers...Enjoy

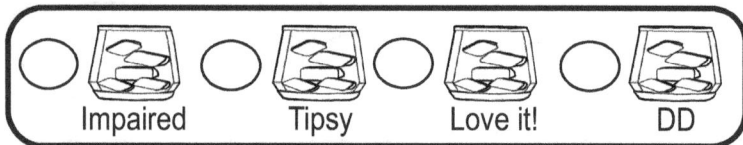

Impaired	Tipsy	Love it!	DD

Slow Down!

- 1/2 ounce of Southern Comfort
- 1/2 ounce of Vodka
- Shot Glass
- Cheers...Enjoy!
- *Deep Breath...1...2...3...*

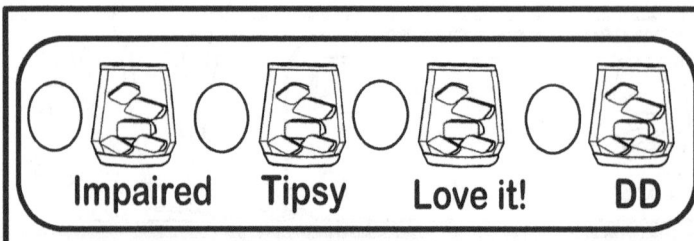

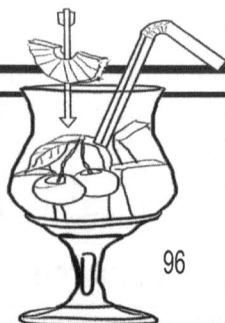

Impaired	Tipsy	Love it!	DD

96

Slippery When Wet

🍓 1/2 ounce of Cinnamon Schnapps
🍓 1/2 ounce of Cointreau Liqueur
🍓 Shot Glass
🍓 Finely Crushed Cinnamon Heart
🍓 *(For Rim of Shot Glass)*
🍓 *Wet the Shot Glass Rim with Schnapps and dip into Crushed Cinnamon Hearts*
Cheers...Enjoy!

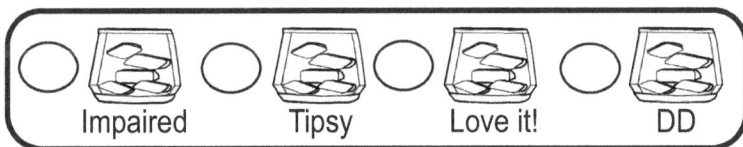

◯ Impaired ◯ Tipsy ◯ Love it! ◯ DD

So Hot!

🍓 1/2 ounce of Drambuie Liqueur
🍓 1/2 ounce of Frangelico Liqueur
🍓 Shot Glass
Cheers...Enjoy!

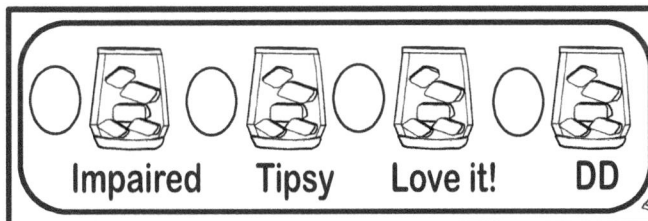

◯ Impaired ◯ Tipsy ◯ Love it! ◯ DD

Don't Drink and Drive Stop

97

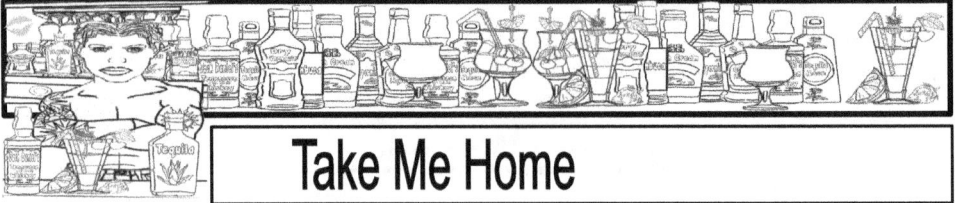

Take Me Home

- 1/3 ounce of Absolut Vodka Citron
- 1/3 ounce of Jon Basil Tequila
- 1/3 ounce of Red Bull (any Energy Drink)
- Shot Glass
  Cheers...Enjoy!

Impaired | Tipsy | Love it! | DD

Tame Me!

- 1/3 ounce of Black Sambuca Liqueur
- 1/3 ounce of Coconut Tequila (1800)
- 1/3 ounce of Johnnie Walker
- Shot Glass
  Cheers...Enjoy!

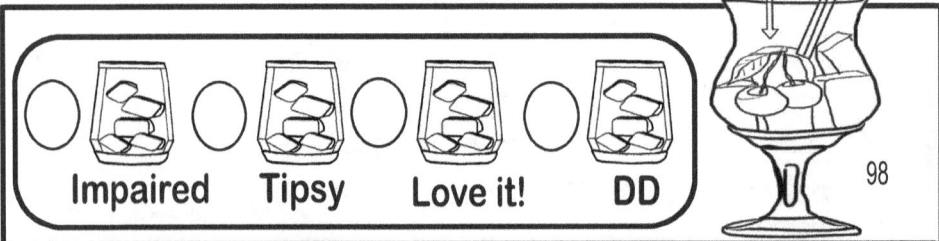

Impaired | Tipsy | Love it! | DD

Tank Top

- 1/3 ounce of White Creme De Cacao Liqueur
- 1/3 ounce of Banana Liqueur
- 1/3 ounce of Tequila Rose Liqueur
- Splash of Grenadine Syrup
- Shot Glass
  Cheers...Enjoy!
  1 Hot Muscular Man

○ Impaired	○ Tipsy	○ Love it!	○ DD

Table Dancer

- 1/2 ounce of Blue Curacao Liqueur
- 1/2 ounce of Banana Liqueur
- Shot Glass
  Cheers...Enjoy!

And 1 Shiny Brass Pole for Dancing

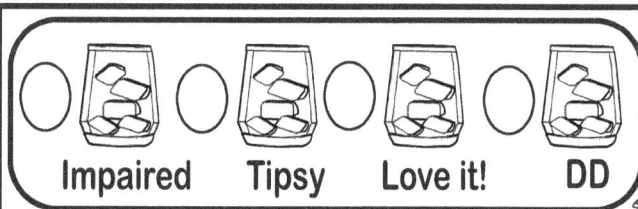

○ Impaired	○ Tipsy	○ Love it!	○ DD

Don't
Drink and Drive!
Stop

99

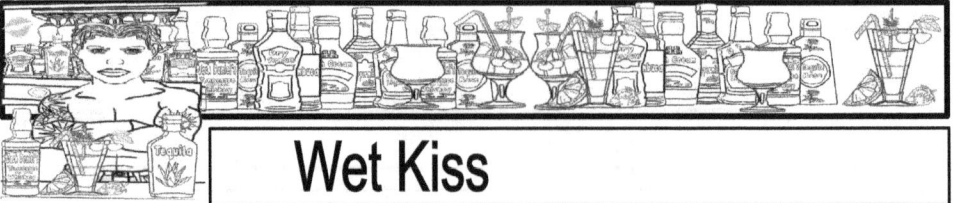

Wet Kiss

1 ounce of Captain's Morgan Spiced Rum
1/2 ounce of Blue Curacao Liqueur
Fancy Ass Cocktail Glass
Add Ice Cubes
1/2 Glass of Sprite
1/2 Glass of Lemonade
Cherries for Garnish
6-10 inch Paper Straw
1 Breath Mint
Cheers...Enjoy!

| Impaired | Tipsy | Love it! | DD |

Wet Willy

1/2 ounce of Sloe Gin Liqueur
1/2 ounce of Silver Tequila
1/4 ounce of Black Sambuca Liqueur
1/4 ounce of Melon Liqueur
Shot Glass
Cheers...Enjoy!
1 Hot Belly

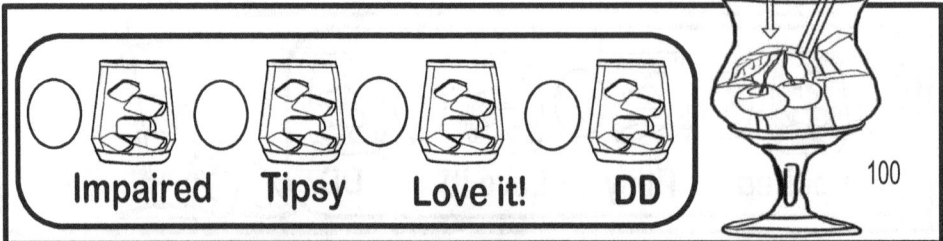

| Impaired | Tipsy | Love it! | DD |

Wet...Wet...Wet

1/2 ounce of Lemon Gin
1/2 ounce of Silver Tequila
Shot Glass
   Cheers...Enjoy!

Impaired		Tipsy		Love it!		DD

Weekend Fling

1/2 ounce of Jim Beam Bourbon
1/2 ounce of Jack Daniel's
Shot Glass
   Cheers...Enjoy!

Impaired	Tipsy	Love it!	DD

Don't Drink and Drive Stop

Weird Martian Hard On

1/3 ounce of Creme de Cacao Liqueur
1/3 ounce of Melon Liqueur
1/3 ounce of Bailey's Irish Cream Liqueur
Shot Glass
Whipped Cream (**on the top of Shot Glass**)
Drizzle of Creme de Menthe on top of
Whipped Cream
Cheers...Enjoy!

Impaired   Tipsy   Love it!   DD

Wall Sex

1/3 ounce of Amaretto Liqueur
1/3 ounce of Bailey's Irish Cream Liqueur
1/3 ounce of Cognac
Shot Glass
Cheers...Enjoy!

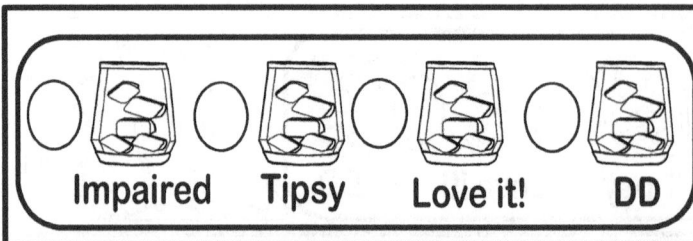

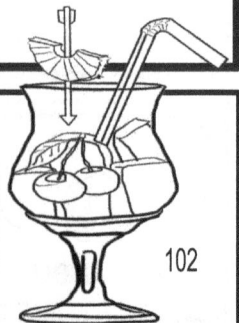

Impaired   Tipsy   Love it!   DD

102

Wild Duck Farts

1/3 ounce of Kahlua Liqueur
1/3 ounce of Bailey's Irish Cream Liqueur
1/3 ounce of Crown Royal Whiskey
Shot Glass
Cheers...Enjoy!

Impaired   Tipsy   Love it!   DD

Wet Cold Nipples

1/2 ounce of Goldschlager Liqueur
1/2 ounce of Bailey's Irish Cream Liqueur
Shot Glass
Cheers...Enjoy!

Impaired   Tipsy   Love it!   DD

Don't
Drink and Drive!
Stop

Wild Twisted Man

1/2 ounce of Fireball Whisky Liqueur
1/2 ounce of Bailey's Irish Cream Liqueur
Shot Glass
Cheers...Enjoy!

○ Impaired	○ Tipsy	○ Love it!	○ DD

X-Ray Me...Fuck!

1/4 ounce of Black Sambuca Liqueur
1/4 ounce of Tequila Rose Liqueur
1/4 ounce of Mozart Chocolate Liqueur
1/4 ounce of Bailey's Irish Cream
Shot Glass
Top Shot Glass with Whipped Cream
Cheers...Enjoy!

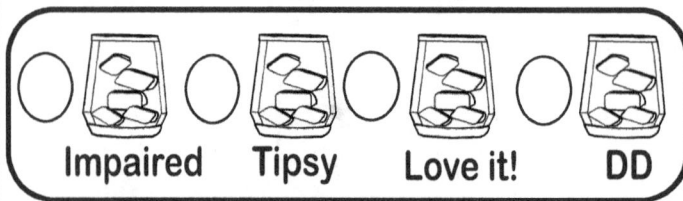

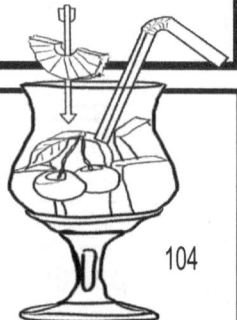

○ Impaired	○ Tipsy	○ Love it!	○ DD

- 1 ounce of Silver Tequila
- 1/2 ounce of Cointreau Liqueur
- Fancy Ass Cocktail Glass
- Add Ice Cubes
- 1/2 Glass of Ginger Ale or Tonic Water
- 1/2 Glass of Lime Bar Mix *(Recipe page-2)*
- Splash of Maple Syrup
- Cherries and Orange Slice for Garnish
- Spear Stir Stick for Garnish
- 6-10 inch Paper Straw
  Cheers...Enjoy!

| ○ Impaired | Tipsy | ○ Love it! | DD |

Zero Fucks Given!

- 1 ounce of Gordon's Pink Gin
- 1/2 ounce of Raspberry Liqueur
- Sexy Cocktail Glass
- Add Crushed Ice Cubes
- 1/2 Glass of Cranberry Juice
- 1/2 Glass of Ginger Ale
- Splash of Apple Juice
- Raspberries and Lemon Slice for Garnish
- Spear Stir Stick for Garnish
- 6-10 inch Paper Straw...
  Cheers...Enjoy!

| Impaired | Tipsy | Love it! | DD |

Don't
Drink and Drive!
Stop

105

Rate your Favourite Cocktail or Shot!

Page

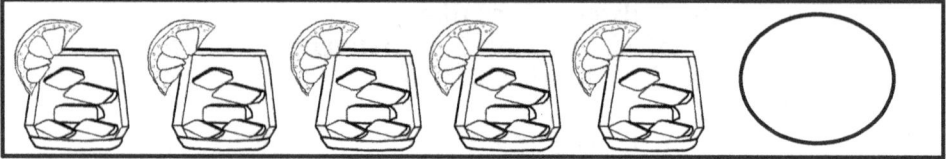

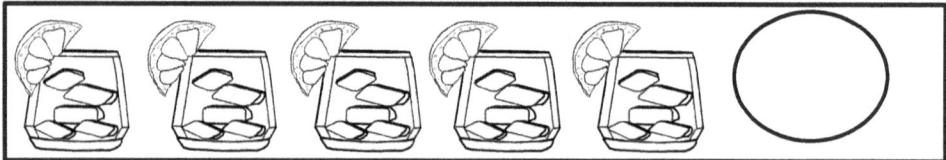

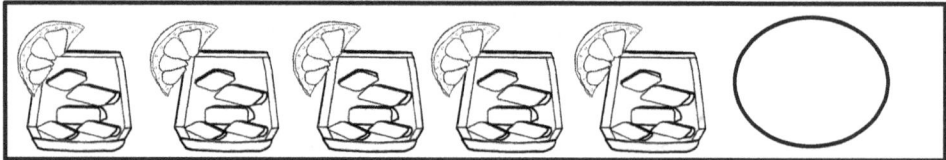

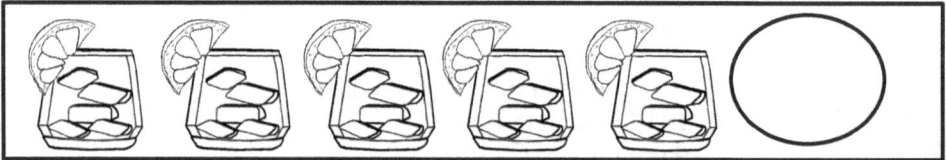

106

Rate your Favourite Cocktail or Shot!

Page

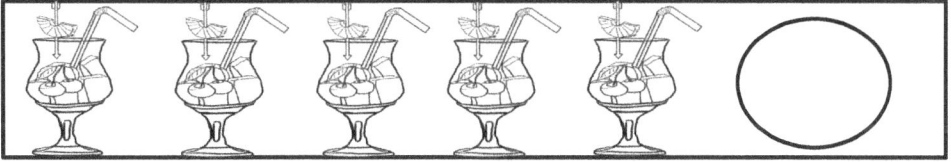

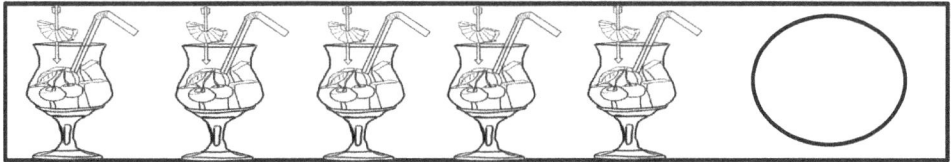

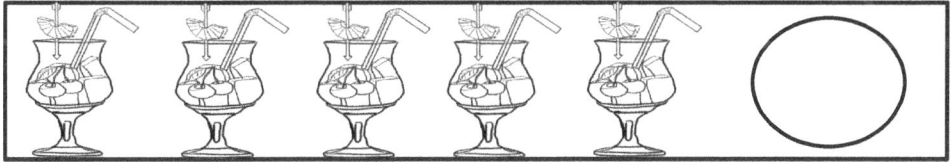

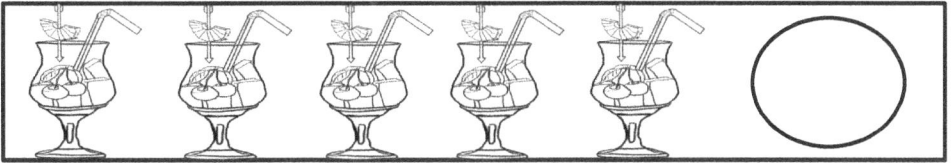

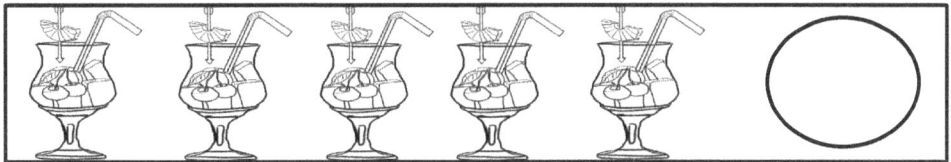

107

Thank You

by Really Thirsty

Don't
Drink and Drive!
Stop

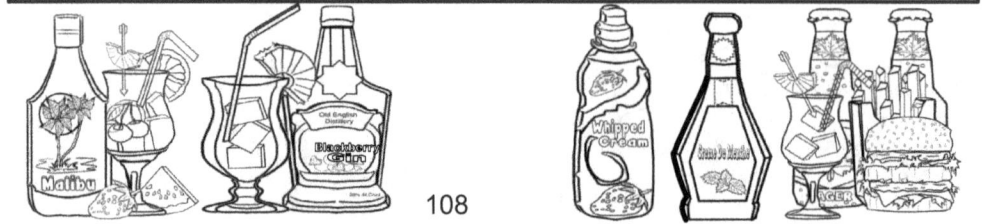

108

www.ingramcontent.com/pod-product-compliance
Lightning Source LLC
Chambersburg PA
CBHW061754020426
42331CB00006B/1477